I0459284

THE BOOK OF GATES

RECARVING the CHRYSOPRASE BOWL

GALLEON

Recarving the Chrysoprase Bowl / Volume 1
The Book of Gates

Copyright 2025 © by Tom McGauley
Afterword 2025 © by Luke Franklin
All rights reserved.

Second Galleon Softcover Edition, December 2025
ISBN 978-1-998122-28-8

Cover photo, Custodio Studio: painting by Alberto Cerritos, acrylic on canvas, from the author's private collection.

Published by Galleon Books
Moncton, New Brunswick, Canada
www.galleonbooks.ca

An early version of this manuscript was published in 1979 by Black Stone Press in an edition of 100 copies.

Library and Archives Canada Cataloguing in Publication

Title: Recarving the chrysoprase bowl. Volume I / Tom McGauley ; afterword by Luke Franklin.
Other titles: The book of gates
Names: McGauley, Tom, author. | Franklin, Luke, writer of afterword.
Description: Includes bibliographical references and index.
Identifiers: Canadiana 20250268094 | ISBN 9781998122288 (softcover)
Subjects: LCGFT: Poetry.
Classification: LCC PS8625.G39 C37 2025 | DDC C811/.6—dc23

THE BOOK OF GATES

RECARVING the CHRYSOPRASE BOWL

VOLUME I

Tom McGauley

Afterword by Luke Franklin

Who know nothing
no reward for them it reads
these have all perished
loves jealousies memory passed out of
nor will they ever play in whatever
is done under the sun

and the girls wail   him
Tammuz   gone
he would have said yes to her
did and is dead
Ishtar bring back this man

a substance around
yew a cloud of light
how does it fight now
how holds he that axe
how pursues he now Persephone sharing

in the spring he will be corn
and apricot blossoming
he will be trout
leap up rainbow
he will be snow out of the lap of
he will be there
birch that maiden leaved
he will be there
love with that sun's warm

held not only in the mind he will be there
I tell him this
not memory but insigned
in that I will see him
consort now of the hidden goddess

In memory of Robert Donaldson Craig.
26 sept LXXII

and justice shall roll down like a mighty water

The Book of Amos

Shirotae   *no*

masago   *no*   *ue*   *ni*

furisomete

omoishi   *yori*   *mo*

tsumoru yuki kana

On   *the*   *pure*   *white*   *of*

the   *sand*   *it*   *has*   *started*   *to*

fall,   *sinking*   *in:*   *just*

look   *how*   *the*   *snow*   *is*   *piling*

up   *deeper than*   *expected!*

Poetry is never writing or books. It is 'voice', *vak*, a still hand that stretches out, all alone. I know this much. Nothing more.

Jayanta Mahapatra.

Recarving the Chrysoprase Bowl.

The Book of Gates.
If only to ourselves we are speaking.
Tuned by Lateness.
This is my way Persians.
After the Qianlong Emperor.
Studies for the Transfiguration.
Buckle snow's fragrant almond cincture.
Lunar Galls.
Towards the Emancipation of the obscure.
Spilling on the linen of capture.
All youngest errs quickest.
Living in the ordinary facts of time.
Lago del Cor.
A venery of Asses.
Koi Ambuscades.
Such nonsense slowly myths blue.
Cerro del Fortín.
Where the green river is.
Ebony Moths.
Who is Nefertem.
Come here lone soldier.
Perseids falling into limitless dark.

I

Flense scriptural from impossible.

Go lunar over what was not said.

Aggravate species boredom

propel dusty candor.

Present-tense licorice jubilees

flense scriptural from impossible.

Never transcend functional utility.

Procrastinate

lucent s-curved apothecary.

Disturbs by pulling into itself all language, all thought

all life disappears. Speech cannot know, cannot speak.

Abyssal, austral, polar, coinciding

Being's black forest retreat

never admitting wars   on the feathered constituency

of the poetic doubt dries. Eyes harden.

Colours limpid, cleaned.

Infamy put away. Words rattle. We are and can only

know in this distance that always *is*

is coming to be

despite engineered forgetting

moves to you

dreams emancipation, health, literacy, not drowned

in suasion, of and by instruments of the conquest.

Matter imagines, wayward, restless, belled, futile,

stupefied, incongruent, yet cannot destroy melancholy

following from Guatemala.

Against a skeptical feather codex dreams condor's wingspan.

Who will spare us from the inexorable?

Moon has come apart.

Does it rain in hell?

Fear's precise colour dims weariness.

Elliptical, muscled, this whispering wets donated entente.

Lick rune stone calming

empty almond shell

    champion

idiom-opened doorway.

Take your silk shirt

from the dresser.

Drenched in filial squalls

why speak at all?

Who would believe

caught brigantine

soon comes to despise

voyage's rigor.

Soluble in moonlight

stone hope

plagiarize gloxinia

anthers cayenne-ish

Twin of demise

appoggiatura

young Werther listen

un-transfigured

gazelles lick salt

from honeyed

slight twine around

your leaping neck

Coppermine River where no tree grows

abrogates gentle sweet Avon

which not only lost but decapitated

blushed a prayer book.

For really the poorest hath a life to live

as does the greatest and therefore truly

every person that is to live

under a government

ought first by their own

put themselves under that

Then I ask where are sweet flowers?

They answer cut whatever you want

drink gently golden hummingbird

who are you looking for?

To the pass Nombre de Dios, iron lances, iron halberds

iron swords, iron shirts, iron helmets, destroy all gods.

In March 800 eaten with chilies.

Omne regnum in se ipsum divisum desolabitur

every kingdom divided

against itself falls to Smallpox Virgin.

Great stones attached

to their feet   whipped as they hung

five thousand tortured, all being idolaters

not possible to proceed juridically against them

impossible to finish in 20 years

Meanwhile all would go to hell

de Landa observes.

That the custodians of a people so new to the faith

should become their executioners.

Whip necessary as bread

El celebérrimo caso de 1562, a three-month Franciscan terror.

They searched his secret chamber,

found small chrysoprase he had not made known

hence sinning against

his profession of poverty.

It was ruled he might not be buried in that cloister

called propriety but planted in a garden.

A thing much talked on as scandalous to all

which they salved

saying he was *outside, beyond, severed from.*

Pectoral diminuendo does not short change

uncurls *postraos aquí la eternidad empieza*

y es polvo aquí la mundanal grandeza.

Untranslatable take off your long pants.

Faith, justice, tibia, carpals, compass breathing.

Long-legged, supine, o your Indian eyes.

That *was* coming

to be our *is*

optimum flatness

roundness

reaching, willing

what binds

the place to others

lost you

somewhere

on Citlaltépetl.

Quick to St Rita's cold creaking pews where throats were blessed

No rainbow's bones caught but walking reverie punished

with Alacoque's Sacré Cœur smothers communards' ashes

  27 May 1871

Ate Pollux, forty francs for his trunk, rats from 60 centimes

bread adulterated catacombs milled bone meal commons ate

  where Sacré Cœur raised up Commune began

Eugène Varlin, bookbinder union organizer shot twice

Twenty to thirty thousand died thus De Goncourt observes

solution brutal but next revolution deferred a generation

Here beginning returned to, only memory can go forward.

Confluent inter-penetrating valleys

to higher mountain villages

houses burning by the

hundreds, glacial terraces

stagger up Zion ridge

Explosion

and his death lift train car roof

Village and river

pine and sawmills, highways and

pilgrimages, spring floods

and funerals

birthdays and twilight woman

carved from a stump

her sculptor rowing out

to save children from drowning.

Intoxicated orchard, lip of childhood

where patriarch hills

reach beyond villages on

the Plain of Consolation.

[In memory of Leonard Mader].

Fill amphora tender warms

Melt liver's sarcasm

Look up from the shattered

Plait amaranth

spill unguent

Fragonard lily

inseparable lip Braille

illegal inmigrante

Monteverdi birch

take your silken straggler

alibis

No truckle bed

Cordelia costs survival

Stage cleared

Adorno, Beckett janitors

where Caesar came

and looked

all the way to the Pacific.

From trawler rolled over in rhythm with

        mortuary ocean

we row across short water home

avoiding wharf's observant civilian patrols

        Beach not far away yields to road

parched fields surround desultory houses

We build small bonfire from oars

        and miserable chattering rest

Barns grayer than remembered

Stoves cold, no food, no newspapers

no belief this the general end

Sodden, exhausted, walking in single file, on guard

        what civil enemy broke the day

breached trawler's attempted flight

to set us on an oppressive short water where

        the drowned sigh around us

and we hope for land again.

Ground mined beneath your feet by a columbine combination

of various men the state

opposes   It is not death caught here below

you eating out your altar Forsythia

criticizes with its periodicity its sublimation of sulfur

its decoration of the liberal desk

Still it is suzerain and exists with its memory

of the pure republic of poetry.

Pliny records the price, a wine dipper of aromatized bluejohn

300,000 sesterces. Such lead to his downfall.

Tigellinus also an experienced voluptuary.

Flavius Scaevinus largely responsible for the betrayal.

Eumolpus poetaster wrote

multos iuvenes carmen decipit

poetry has deceived many a young man

putavit se continuo in Heliconem, who thinks

he's immediately arrived, who scans in elegant paraphrase.

Naked on raven's back ask what of England dies with him?

What darkened with Gloucester's bloody eyes?

Who will leave Ireland again for this fortified new world wilderness?

To persist is to admit defeat's regularity.

Where is death tonight?

Why are paths emerald in their wrestled paradise?

Cut at clement, none step by unsaid.

Not more now because of a few poems, what a clipping says.

Night soughs *why this place where no fauns come?*

Wasted, wasted, all letters lie.

Scatter aurora borealis' quetzal plumes

steal the consolation colour is.

Among the trees one bird sings

knowing made no stone's silence wiser.

Copper feral tenderness jilts clumped sedge

       timothy holds

pollination in abeyance.

Dress in hyperbole meadowlark keens.

Crooked Beak Crying to Heaven

a deeper economics shapes

our shamelessly inadequate strength.

Homeric in more than gesture

     we anger not ripen

hence these theorems hummingbird pierces.

He said fart like Dante, England a grave of poets.

He will not be duped despite blue cloth

      above his rotten knee.

Tammany gloire, what will your name be?

      Sleeve of fog moves down your belly.

Pre-empt buddy system jive, pull cantilever

eat with nine green sticks, lame greed.

Classical unmasked is what they all want.

      Slip out of your shirt.

Set and rise again, ride to Cloud Mountain.

      With reluctant homeopathy

American whiskey promotes pale squalls.

As if anyone could refuse visibility

or ungracious, amend prosecuted hunger.

But in his dream a strange animal and minutes later

at the fire his nose bled.

No one could stop it.   Friends assembled   one burnt his nose.

Was he alive, scar still visible. His mother wept, he asked her *stop*.

They had slept in the path of swaiaswax *who travels on fixed routes.*

He lay in darkness, suffered in sunlight.

Inside his head he heard a bee, words of his song brought to him.

She spoke his name. He shook his hands as if to dance.

II

Leukanthes.

Right laments the passing of a time

when youths were disciplined, modest

leukanthes, white-flowering

melikhrous, honey-skinned.

As Socrates reminds Glaukon

who as an *erotikos* should remember:

if they're dark say they're manly

if fair, children of the gods

who get under your skin.

When an athlete got up

he had to brush the sand

take care not to leave an imprint.

Who had put thigh forward

not to show anything *cruel* or *harsh*

adjectives predicated of Eros himself.

Right's point sight torments.

Where Plato broods, eremenos rested.

You came secretly, sent a poem.

I answered do you see this

Then I was quiet.

Lie down in wild meadow dialect

rocket-saint under jerkin.

Crackled skepticism allows

wistful single recessional

demurely slip into yellow sweater

deliberately bevel chrysoprase.

Polish bones

hunt sour sigh

Year 5

3rd month

of summer

day 9, silver

falls

in flakes

Open tomb

alabaster

sleeps

night longer

than Catullus

suspected.

Alone you are

a well

double you

are time.

Fetter stutter's triste jestering

Adieu fond grim harlequin

Brandish delight, never death

    Harvest itching rose

give four moments of relief

then retire, mirthful gladiator

        of swallows

Alone in broad noise

      horse charge rebuttal

Take baroque plantation ivory

make twelve green bones stand up

Steal coherence from the rain

    Teem with umbilical treachery

re-asserting triomphe

caesarean in equanimity.

There a river from a desert, nonetheless fluid, broad-banked

templed, commercial, full of vegetarian silt. In its

attendant monuments bulls tick-free sacrificed

un-tasted supple menhirs, black to tail

        fertile as a Nubian smelter.

There a river hoarded weathers and in this fierce sun

condor, cobra, shape alliance.

There a river interminable, bending

along the Libyan plain where it shouldn't

abolishes, befriends impossible, flows on forever.

       Here speech begins within copper wires

not sarcophagus stairs fine-boned brown feet climb

     trailing quetzal's aurora.

Nor where delicate tongue twists past juniper lips.

Speech begins in desertion, detains absence

slaked such that retribution off stage

rakes charred bones of victors.

      With tendril tenderness

speech seizes cold chaos where all surges.

Wet Alhambra stamen

adjacent completion

harden executed dahlia

Cottonwood helot

Moorish honeysuckle

cloister in meteor

shower's jasmine arms.

Canals cleared, new fire started

Feathered provincial styling

raised to fluorescence

Oaks keeled brought smallpox.

Later, sea otter rain-proofed

Cantonese, as lascar

menaced japonica.

Creosote settles

over spited solstice.

Whole peoples disappear.

Languages, cities

jungle overcomes.

Death of meadowlark

remote, exilic, adamantine

placates this fretted staccato.

Distance it, it distances the only.

Magnificat

podzolic

susurration

exultate

9 morpheme

shadow

-infolded

motley

the Dance

of the Old Men

ourselves

huaraches

slapping.

Small finches, sparrows, juncos embroider sparse

branches with chirrupy discourse.

Profit made mountain undo itself.

Copper first magic, then came zinc

    lead and silver, then smelters.

Acacia signified pollution reversed.

      Wasted years accrue.

What had we done? Desire uncovered

made public, no succinct

answer, nor chanting minor poets a garland.

Labeled *first century Roman small Apollo*

or *hermaphrodite unsatisfactorily reconstructed*

partial left skull missing

          to you come girls

     with offerings singing in the last

of empire, baskets of onions, melons

       bundled troves of basil.

Each formed stillness aches forward.

Not honeyed adoration nor to excite

but because air knows only words

   carry truth girls are, allows sinewy

lithe tight-shaved youth roughly caress despite

     merciless centuries.

Bronze androgyne correct

    terrible conquered daylight

With same song reproach Saturn at his meal.

    Such an enemy curdles forgetting.

Throat thrones, quetzal feather rests now

      reposes on this earth.

Despite currency failure, collapsed earth at Hokkaido

                    encrusted lamentation

exaggerated white garden of theory taunting insufficiency

patrician boredom's obstetric fist

        suppress nothing.

Molten wind envelops protestant poplar.

Iris speaks, *take my hand.*

          No futile river crossing here.

Awaken reassured desertion no option. Savored

trembling eyelids replace treasure stolen.

At corridor's end nothing. Illusion broken into

plundered. Cut anklets for orphan smallest creeks choir.

          This lip should, lisping, poplar

Brabant, fall over a peripheral invasion of England.

         Not twilit gods but Orkney ossuary.

Silted commons show raven summons dolphin-ridden delphinium.

         There everything else lay.

Barely a dust mark left on the shelf where late mannerist notes

struck embargo ice, ruining musty flight.

Ethics require broad hairy antennae. For a farthing exhume

sparrow's prickly *sweet murmur.*

Wild gorse hints moths morganatic downstream

swarm. Not milt but fluted raggedy invariance exits.

Rhapsody *tremuloides* renews auroch's ruddy brown,

cerise pens fill lit cressets,

streaked cirrus dries on lunar table.

False pastorals employed by king, party or state,

mercenary, inductive expressionist

malaise, dusk-naked, play days-done dominion.

Where broken spear hushes, hyacinth

bleeds, anthracite boundary remains uncrossed.

House Flemish repetitions gallant,

husband Pliny's *red spicy bark.*

Lips' friction a lewd fricative pulls back the clamor of

heroic music, be it anthem, bellyache or evensong.

A muddy pal never slights with russet but whispers the Scottish tragedy.

Divergent kinship chauffeurs, art laws retrofit

    Velázquez's lace cuffs helm need to arise to secret

glass wages. Red crayon master fools molded golden flourish.

    Dispute all of everything, justice faults violently.

Only you hurt ivory. Frugal as a raven morning

        chestnut blossom triages bulldozer slope.

Yet French liberty craved scraps with the formalism of an empty hand.

Abscond absence, wormwood from imperfection

Remission swallows reminiscence.

Withhold yourself, wipe away forbearance.

That abundance alludes to acacia thorns.

Contrarily pronounce *achadomye*

Doctor Johnson would accent first syllable.

Be sharp in the Land of Shinar

agree to resemble speed, song added.

Passerine hedge sparrow sing with another.

Heave accidie, hawk ascending

embrace around the neck confederate.

Accuse headless crustaceans

They acknowledge no superior.

Remain quiet, adapt umpire apron.

Maidenhair adieu to adjacent

day commander admit

adolescent bricks nourish Adonis.

Adrift betake yourself to another

Overshadow sunburnt brown arrival.

Beloved adversary turn your attention

give notice innermost municipal magistrate

shield Aeolian copper from theories of the beautiful.

[Aeolian Copper].

Eleison-desperate enfold

bare-chested

small-cocked dahlia.

Anti-pastoral

praise stillness.

Accelerated

oneiric, lucid

pensioned desperado

mollify

strident small

champing plenitude.

There is no alternative.

Killed by stupidity

alive by it as well

stupid made, undid

but saved

everything

agonizingly restarted.

Black coral obelisk refracts sky-born smell.

Revolutionary romantickal

misses all Roman makeovers.

Where sleeve rubs, sell muscled prime.

Sneezing emerald in skimpy white t shirt

Taiwan tip toes and from him mutation

    of Persephone's names.

Fugitive verbs lick assassin

ascend insinuation's *histoire de vente*

    scrape semen's restriction.

Flutter slain tone, foment nectar's compassion.

To eat you alive, turned inward

essay creation, diaphanous your boots.

    But you knew all along you would not refuse.

Let me smell your hands, full of *take me fragrant star.*

Nuzzle abundant in the small of his back.

Brocaded bells lisp chaste as laughter.

Ovid's gabled pessimism sniffing, pawing

torments assurance.

Who will tell gamelan play *Chemise of April.*

Some of Paris revolted.

Shinobu, supple, without detractors

a fennel musk, constantly boned hurly burly.

You pile salt to envelop bulls' flesh but not before bees find lost hive.

Fluctuating Hesperides tangle begats, unknot pearly everlastings.

Starlings, ravens, fill presiding oaks with chutter.

Tall-eyed dandelion, almond-poached porphyry eyelash

comfort hermitage, every tool a die, every fool a sty.

Might quick shadowy poesie reproach Castile

conquer pedestrian, rebut baroque, indent emerald.

Do not explain anything.

Lady Murasaki's long line reaches beyond September.

Four cinders of hope articulate amigo.

Resisting division coherence

means separation. Count

embarkations, radiant minute advertise

mirthless *pirámide escrita*. Shirt the wind.

In gold lean back from salt cellar

Hips salacious crinkled

touch finale impress

un-degraded Monteverdi play.

   Through split lip

crystal tube with

hummingbird feather, here

anonymous conqueror vanity sharpens.

Henge later carved by Apelles, small purple grapes

burst from marble cool hand.

Lynx steps, growls, then ivy over evinrude.

A subaltern Ciceronian twilight falls.

Weirs memorize flows sweetened with alyssum.

Pungent as blooded moor cock, or in britches

asleep, sleek boxer inside

the large outside sound of rain breathing.

III

Riper than a pear.

Indian agent wrote what she was doing

a policeman took off her clothes

   found a man so they gave

her a suit, cut off his hair.

When I saw him again he was

   no more my sweetheart.

Can't you see he's riper than a pear

    no use anymore

and the women say *o dear*

Philinos, your pretty flowers are drooping.

Perfect proportion in plain stone

sarcophagus, champion, pentathlon

four horse chariot race, boxing

received 140

     amphorae of olive oil inscribed

I am a prize of the games at Athens.

     Did not specialize

skill not from brute strength.

Not particularly robust

five feet seven inches tall, not

handsome, large nose, perfect teeth,

died age 40, cause unknown.

And so to bed, beans tossed out the window

stove ashes emptied

in uphill garden's bright blue morning.

Father absent, a bit of death in the deal.

You gave away cow and milk for a few beans?

Giant upstairs could be no worse

than her anger, her reproach

about *delicate*, dreamed, spelled or written.

Jack of airy trades

an introspective jerk this Jack but a climber.

Leave alone these improvident sales.

In vulgar eloquence repeat such

gulled again, in an economy of painful mystery

I, Jack, so attest.

With a feminine ending dawn converts sullen path

through up and over any rocks to defeat intoxication.

Hence heart never ages beyond repair.

But his feet slip into girl's shoes, in your hair barrettes.

Lean, slender *el payaso* celebrate a thousand indifferences.

Retract into dominance, softly suck smoky lips

Shoulder into black stone lisping darkness honed.

Into flat cold impressed, lip, lip, lip, lightly.

At Dipolog flood

silts shivering

children,

Josephina, grits

fish head broth

shredded ginger.

Dapitan, rain.

Tep Peng, Ilocos Sur

flagrant kingfishers

a conversation

about

galaxies then sleep.

Zealots threaten and swear they would rip up his bowels

besides many other villainies they could not in truth perform.

Ill-tempered expands, December amends *who am I?*

American cousins play Barbary baseball, write clan magazines

in the cinema pretend

they are still called Junior, afraid dark merlin

a little winged knife cuts up the sky. Move

along cilantro pew ridge Meriwether expanded.

Rome looted laws Catullus replaced.

Bedouin what does ocean drift shape?

Bring emperor to disintegrated stammer.

Disarm space boy, silver fuck mayonnaise.

Luther speaks death's nibbling bite children

refute looking for Atlantis. Hoodlum world our home is far away.

From El Retiro's Atget-perfect lake

thence to Mérida , missing Cortez'

Medellín and into cool August's Lisbon

Later cromlechs and Irish rain

All the while Lesbia's sparrow pecks

pumice smooths his pretty new book

Bosch's nun-hooded hedgehog natters

        what chirrup

guessed, yellow, sweet, ensnaring.

Yellow wears slippery shoes, an unhappy god.

Will Watson be eaten by the painted shark?

Expose juniper's indifferent root. Loft enigma.

Foofaraw say of Plautus'

devising, glad plumy benefice scattered without

combustion glowers,

                marigold all along.

February ignition, mucilaginous haecceity's feldspar

Longinus' styptic calendula *ha ha*

ha frequently obtrudes following moody feints.

Though mountain disagree, hushed *siempre*

        blunts impediment.

Obvious martyred snowdrift kitsch stipples precious

lumpen. Grinning centurion reached what rebus released

        old bugger's witty toenails.

We have arrived slain twee nightingale.

Erasmus, stealthily

Friday's Mahler

a white rump

Plutarch records

books chinampa

nopal with eagle

sssssssssss

Ophidian Baltic

malvaceous

Dioscorides

pohickory hidalgo

Blouse from Bontoc,

pig feast in held up

open palm to sky

hand of the world

we could not leave

unless gone

before sunrise

on the day of her

burial, Bauko.

Slender blue thing

lost participle

wallop attentive

death

Slip ladder away

Golden snare

you are one

unsubordinated

Hanuman's.

Who cares if it is music no one talks about

Poise pointillism over heroic poke-pudding

Hellebore saved lunch time

Rudder stirs up muddle

    Clover bell on the wrist

dandelion dressing elevator door

All bid for market share

Lynx pads over watercress haecceity

Herded nonchalance humid hinds come

    skimming in the door left open

by an antique god of earthquakes.

Now must I part from you, a small rope, a tiny ladder

a leaf of turquoise, las rosas de Castilla, and amble out

towards fireweed barrow set with equinox willow.

With mountain goats' wool, clematis bag withstands

a hundred pounds, carries all of fallow summer.

Stray there, delphinium glimmers, larkspur nearby.

In the room of the dissolution of matter

advise debt-slaves peppermint often follows.

Not Calvinist, but on the balcony boys lick pointed ovaries

IV

Fatwa thrown out the window.

Young Adam

non-two-ness

all radio

may x

remain mortal

caliph casteless

Ayatollah

bhakti sweeper

Marxist funeral

worker

dharna

or sit down!

equal to 4 cubits

integrates

ego-extinction

fatwa thrown

out the window.

That problem remaking

    Armorica jistens

Fie high bred tkkk tkkk tarryum

Youse mansorial

      youse escobarbative

youse scouse tawny rempel

    bland hoopoe

anarcho-nimbus circulo-stratified

with doobey

    doobey differentiation

    on the castrate grayerling

you surd surgeon experimalleee

"Me ontic slippable," Headrex and Virid speak.

Headrex:

Yup I a yaller yeller doggist

downhill

jammer jamboree

But clefts and ditches mine I mine

Preformative yip yip yippee

not wind broken but ditheree

dithy rammed

a bit obsmoktious

Yes, puor in spirit, poor in breath,

breezy me ontic

slippable in or over easy

Virid:

Mock me snot

Headrex:

Yu've weird puller portal shot your crank

Virid:

I bearish knock knee

not marmoreal moulou

but molly transmuttrified

knock knot nilly you've

pluvialities wettened

Headrex:

What waits 'll be bumfry

but thou Portobello

thou Schlumpf not yummery

but two kirbys sayd jerky

automated hospicery

yum telling your final

Virid:

Snot drugger

you are overdropper

ortho my lecturer in

doune und daid

what sails you saidering?

Headrex:

I tall handsome won

weightery

I tall prick prickee

you bourne-borne

my porcee poached

neanderthick

But tum tum tummeree

me be quoits and maybe

pied jellyniferous

Boyd barber be off your turf

Virid:

Too good quick lumpy

tupper-scared

you grumble

too mightily mulch

Headrex:

But basics buoy

our buy out

Hour sublime

that choppin block

of neat's licure

lovable your lickorish

Virid:

Glim me in the gloamin

Stand there you stewart

headless squirrel

Let me measure you

neckless heliopompous stop

your ranging

Breaded weal lines up

with theorem's offer

Yours expert liturdgical noise

Headrex:

But siring aurora all is on vanes

Towards me angrified mourning

reddens peaked

Envoys bus older ire

for apple-less morn

Shrine cannot leer

reading vanity's

precipice cogitandi

Virid:

Cheap chips chill penurhea

gorge ictus

Nobel rarin to forego

an amorite's fantastic mopery

shamed futtocked tuthill

grated enormousies

Headrex:

Stop iananing even to a degreek

of finical femincy

Pin a prynne

into his elaborating pyx

Delicaseys or frumey fustiness

cannarded overbright

Sir Jenry Fulsome

nee quadruplicate tous alliances

Virid:

But I rust I smut

I overweighty languish

joiled jalousie spume

I sire dents de lion

And the likeable canoe

thou coffee rain buckram

disarsterer

Headrex:

Costain comestable constrain me

from admission

The merry you gettifried

an obregon steals my let

in Texarkana

medicates me rostrum

So many dominos

prust prussic prooshan

to the hilt

Jacks a yerpy little

victorine stetson

to wherry and geek

Virid:

Shut the stump up you hoosecow

Little bratacious recombine

your jeans mitt son pulchritude

Slide tongue to coifed interjoint

Bend mitre nigrescent

Suckle him swill him swivvers

Slip skivvies from nun cullum

from grief and pressure washer

Bold your starry flame

to his buttering foal

Stoat will reverie cunt him literary

till he glags

Not stomp him silly

you trot of faulty tribalese

Headrex:

Come doune, come doune

you stilly mugger

Ore costical come down

Fire-haled bartel of waterifery

call flire fire, cross

to Peter's house organically

In your ample hand ignoramus

dumb avec indillation.

Fall away from their blockade, brick wall

bar goons, ordinary grudge fests

    unremittingly violent

Fall into Tin Cup rapids

    where Old Woman of Dried

Bracken rescues you

    fromfader urer ðu arð ðu bist in heofnum.

Healing quixotically all heart's ships fiercely sailing,

what we turn to, friends, daily bread

whiff of dubious peony, starry eyebrow mistress

      a pertinence unquestioned bends

 to offer cockerel witness.

However sated we bargain wilting futures

calyxes entwined with russet.

Such our days, stealthily alone, viperish yet abraded

breathing afternoon's tall iota, plural, identical, endless

just short of a small eternity,

      without much patience

too easily angered

loving justice's rare present tense,

saboteurs awaiting sharp hoarse metallic call of flicker

      beg with impertinent

sincerity a certain confidence along

marigold-scented walkways as we repair homeward,

where are you?

Milky allium

Endymion's

sleeping bribe

hung on

silver hook

clover's

Here there

are heroes.

Into these palatial commons, these meadows clever

these spelunkered sentenced draperies

angst christened graciously

with eudaemonics and pitched contraries

      yet spelled into jasmine ordinands

veering through and away from Giottoesque space.

      Taking transatlantic *rebelde* peregrination

consulting all the almanacs of average fatality

a vocabulary struggling

into secular space back to the foisted present

 a clawed-out niche

    of spoiled hoping contentment

snuggled into as inquisitor's poor relatives set

      out from Herculaneum

keepers of an uplifted genocidal civil engineering.

Let it go. Little else to do but return what bouquet, what banquet.

Fault Caesar. Link termite to religious undercover.

Full of boredom embalm halcyon.

Alberta disappears

Commune eats its predicate, saxifrage rider lost his way.

Migratory demotic pulling right ambles

to snide kingdom come.

Callow summer distill this dearest glittering abdication.

What is conceded never subsides.

Let world proceed to its ruin, unexpected hand

refit copula's shoulder. Threshing starry Bedouin

cobble with cocklebur crutch's fertility.

Stygian ireful sinners promenade finely in big black shoes.

Hunger drove pure assault

on this pre-owned wilderness.

Leap back against the pricks and carnivores. Whoever

wiped away luxury's smile drinks thee up.

formosae vincla puellae

et sedeo duras ianitor ante fores

Bound fast in the bonds

of lovely I sit a janitor before

his stubborn doors

Lured, tawny, dazzled, sleeve's

lost echo

blood-murmur striking zero

shaded slowly that bright comes.

Raft serene past gentile persuaders.

Previous brightness disabled excelsis, Valla

       wrecked pious code

sky anther befiddled *demos*

silver lacrimae loosened consternation

Thence headaches all down the valley.

Alluvial lubricates loblolly, fools weed prevalence.

    Dreary pan smacker dredges

locust forest pine beetles rampage.

Northern obscurantist dooms bright prediction.

Alevin lute loots and nobody cares.

                But meadow

lushly light, explosive art fails

its own allegations.

Compensatory sails catch warm green wind.

Winter's thrall hides inside early summer,

condemns these lengthy side-trips.

This he

is here

Or amidst

those things

this person

coming

to be ever

ungraspable

but grasped

held

as water,

ear in the

sky

of a word

caught in

bronze

he leans.

Running away, breaking all that is not strong enough for you,

   honest as ever, you would

not take, giving back little but everything,

your shifting momentary offer of nothing in return.

Then to the other side of the Ganges,

     to the Kali of a 1000 hands, the Botanical

Garden's giant lily pads and the naming of a child Kayva Alma.

Then pandals with Kali's bloody heads,

necklaces and song and midnight tea

in the streets of Kolkata brought by Sudam

     whose door opened

and there were little lamps flickering in every doorway.

     [for Kalaivanan of Thanjavur].

Remain the sufferers, the gullible

the splitters and the always dreaming awake who

would be led by chimney angels.

Himmelstrasse an entirely different matter

amounting to the disqualification of Europe

in the High Court of Hell.

I am the hidden broken cup he says, naked raw light,

sweet jaggery bundled.

I am the useless, the unknown, the ill-informed

who shall come leaping with dark eyes,

with the blue throat of uninjured truth.

Such shall be the broken handles, the rhyme of yearning.

Mine he says is dark like the silence

of whirring grasshopper night. Feel his strong arms,

who gives honey to the mouth

of river's unsatisfied longing. It sustains it does this emerald plantain,

this stick of gunpowder, this roll of mitigated pleasure.

Such gives the brown-faced thambi,

the famous one of repenting peppercorns

and the ardor of cardamom's soul

Such the fleet arrow sharp, flung up.

Such the man who trades away

copper for the sight of the daffodil-tongued one.

Such is absence formed from hope's nothing.

Such the legend of the false cinema of significant insults.

Such the merit of his arrival.

V

Eternity craved and thwarted.

Torrent's silt of longing,

rice terrace rising, winnow of alder, breeze

        of dismissal,

all sharpen adze's dumbed morning

Littered with cardamom or mint

be it wave-ripped to firmly furious against

decay marbleized, the impossible

     bowels to liver

stains love's lost nape, crow's proudest

    flight away from

  into pinkish resemblance

of eternity craved and thwarted.

All had been written, had been said, was sufficient

All was its all, was its own, was total yet remained silent, curvaceously

hanging in the branches.

In the letter he wrote to his superior he re-

iterates the brutality he suffered at the hands of his fellow travelers

who begrudgingly took him and carried his carnivorous soul

into the longhouses of their warrior cruelties.

She wrote about those who lined up, awaited execution

hearts ripped out by priests of the hummingbird god.

sour milky

rough-tailed

unbrambled

Golconda's

mined

slipping

black rod

sky-dressed

how you

sparkled

first time

I saw you

Four evangelists

evaporated close to Creston.

It was three o'clock.

But plumbers more

importantly took their wrenches

opened jakes

of ordinary flowing verbosity.

Cow

jumped over the moon.

Absence never severed from

      harbinger inescapable

 only ever memory, tribune and strength

visible over all these years and days

creation's feather of doubt quelled

      yet inscribed *vividly mine*

gracious desire's enduring marker make

densely handwritten shadow

     speak and form

one name written with two falcons

           [For Scott Westgate].

You leave Hotel Harlem Nocturne,

white-haired, shamanic, alight horse,

      breathing mote,

excited crossbow, 1000 year twilight.

     Not held in a small book

  or empires of frozen

Nakhi juniper, ride in from the great desert

at the far corner of our land

existence will not

      encumber you again.

Exhume me, polish my bones

wrap me in birch bark, carry me to

the long house of your mother where your sisters

play dice with my bones while you sleep.

    I wanted to be your constellation

you corroded me with anger

made me count and beg like a sparrow.

    How I want to forget you.

Abasement excites judgment. Graves

fall upside down, pears ripen again.

Compañera poesía, a cleft in handsome.

blonde, bare, dappled, marauding,

the wound is perfect.

In the white garden of theory

in compartments of amaryllis's heart

      taunted by insufficiency

hungered to our very medieval pores

it is difficult, no impossible, to concede this defeat.

Subtle distinctions between affection and fatality

      are distractions to be forgotten.

Desire steps through itself onto a continent of wars

previous, present and postponed.

      Take the English traveler at his word

Come into the high village of the pectorals

Set moon back into its colonial portrait.

We anger not ripen

Hence these theorems' bright monism made *no*

stone's silence wiser

yet took copper from our shadows.

      I am not Simonides, do not

remember where the poets sat when roof fell in on them.

Like the best of places has no

      real location yet is everywhere

along this coast in the wake of war canoes.

We sought cloves, burnt the usual

villages, tired Christ

already repackaged desiccation.

Such rutting imperfections

carried forth from Ithaca.

We are

or might be

what forest

is dreaming

we are

walking

we are

attracted

I speak

to his father

I am a janitor

I say.

With slow hands flake out basaltic chair of soft dark.

Let me collect you in your raven clothes.

Morning hail comes down like shot.

Dreary formalism of azure, pure republic of

   poetry, rainbow bag with a hole in it

from which nothing is lost, Hölderlin's limping post-

stile-moderno cancels, elevates, preserves.

Sparrow hawk's voracity tests sky above

Noake's Road. Trade, god and smallpox left

fortified upriver villages empty, Kitselas

   Canyon, 1832. Cowboys, Americans,

ruined not only the land its arteries the imagination

we fight for, the poets were also defeated.

Moon slips into the land a brother haunts.

Yellow porcelain speaks against our sorrows,

our False Dimitis. Astride a house of

discourse, wooden-carved, osprey-winged,

want caverns demand, farms absence,

  overcomes remembrance,

almond shell's emptiness a flower form of snow.

You air, you forest dark with

bristled alder and hawthorn,

you tender dogtooth violet

    no hurt here inheres.

We have been taught

older we are cut away.

Here we have played

    nor shall stop,

there is death in that.

    Washed we are

and dare such trespass

out of body whisperings

to the one lost in the night

do not come in the

    evening rain

celadon is no excuse

you are a gracious danger.

Mice eat secrets of the spirit

morning shrieks warning

idle rhyme cannot

find its home

silence crosses

the face of the moon.

Our loves are revenge.

There is a deeper

economics shapes

our shamelessly

inadequate strength.

Armed we have warned far

more than the logic

of star led men

or clerks of mediocrity.

Radiant gleaming city, burnt

by your pitilessness.

To reproduce

is

is no

sophist joke

but as close

as air is to is

is

is enough

is

is always.

Fervent adheres,

chance overthrows,

war skids

into kitchen suddenly

drying cardamom

hips, steel rounds

flake caliph's dome.

Who never was

cannot abscond,

waits as

memorial berm,

so that ribcage

carry rate of village

after village slaughtered.

In the white room prepare

ephedra for wakefulness, carry

      pomegranate wood

spread southward plaids and twills

Shy away as you see everything

      built into the ocean

gradually vanishing.

At the festival of the death

      of flowers

sharp points on her wings

    her obsidian edges

the forensic probe of her tongue

re-particles the practical.

Pitt gets the deal and Florida Blanca

    the language to allow

no northern boundary, and

the Peruvians and others

find Nootka no place to grow

and Meare's lies discovered to

be in reality lesser

    than he claimed

and the house not as grand but

a few wretched planks, so careen her

    over on the beach,

plug her with spruce pitch and sail away.

Girls' voices

through black

jade night

Whole world rotting

starry fortress pillowing

Tear away from

yet replenish great

chrysoprase

commandments

of Heraclitus

With the stars moaning

take two horses where

10 centuries earlier

four hundred thousand fell.

Then a boy on horseback

offers woven basket

for found bit of metal.

Catch cinnabar river-stone

To the trees of Tuscany

and the now refugee-crowded

beaches of Sicily, resist

Propose, re-sole wordy

not yet winded passion.

Spread the tent of memory

in the garden

of the Villa Medici

Find three-spined wolf-fang

Blacken azure indifference.

Hard, diurnal, cretaceous

the pink-walled arroyo

of the blue desert

of his final crossing

to the requisite

but fading city of empire.

dusk to red dawn cedar

precious alley

with the girth of Orion

plunge unheard

unbidden, unheralded

unknown, not stilled

restless as a monkey

king in Lanka.

VI

Luxembourg gardens after dark.

Wigmakers, carpenters, silk workers under trees on

        the Champs-Élysées, cooks, hairdressers, jewelers

shoemakers, painters, sculptors, glaziers

Count Despaulx dressed in frock asked a

      Swiss Guard to take a stroll.

Marquis de Saint-Clément takes unemployed 19-year-old

        into the trees. Priest Mathurin Dupuy,

Luxembourg gardens after dark, 30 July 1781, La

Petite Bergamotte, La Petite Troteuse, Le Breton

La Picarde from the provinces, hold

       each other by the hand, arm in arm

have sex on the spot, 18 July 1782, would have a

lot of pleasure together he said

offered 12 sols, Foucault sent him to prison.

Sucked jeweler's several times, put his bowels into

and told not to say anything to mother or

      priest. There was nothing wrong

with what they did since his confessor undoubtedly did the same.

        [after Merrick]

Dear Reynolds love that black kylix era.

In Sais saucers of salt and oil burn.

But what do they say? *Never?*

Sleeping wetness knows but cannot warn.

 Liberty spreader is beaten back

by shepherd's spoon.

Like now it was October

and polygamist memory

wold not aryse and flee the thinges that delighted.

Soft old gigolo Saint John on a small stool pours coffee

laced with cinnamon and searches with hands of smoke

      Five times damned flex lickable.

Too good for god freeze in cello's reach

Blousy paper-whites implicate

            else sheened

by Degas' yellow beguiled meadow balks

        Try viburnum ginger

Narodnaia sotsial'naia utopiia

in the blinded building of crackled stairs.

Thomas Gage to England

7 January 1637

26 silver beaks well-wrought

screaming

slaughtered for no reason

entrails blush

his friarly practise

at stake two burned alive

golden

leek

Oblate

anal

ichthys

plunder

catch

caught

flutes

broken

imagen

de bulto

1556

800 000

dead

in

your hair

behind

Cerro

San

Cristóbal

collapsing

palomino

duende

veritas

fer

de lance

besieged

by

cicada's

whir

Raft into light blue weightlessness

Before the accidental moment

we knew no better hence were immune.

Pandemos protect magistrate's

recovery at Nauplia's spring.

Thence to Luca, Pisa, Arezzo,

then a chateau in the Aquitane.

More photos in London,

in shower, in jockstrap.

Gliding soft fern astronomy

dell deft clover, a perfect apparition

a query in the house of silent ushers.

Anti-chafing cream on pursed

Cantonese lips, flirting heart

severed from mannerism

One or more delicious

on the downs

slow and soothing

each letter a fine snow

carried rivers in its deepening.

bow drawn back

lilium columbianum, tiger's, sue

the stars for your estate

gold stud in your ear

oil your acoustic

       passage

bebop candor feminine

yes, the one in your hands.

sugar

mountain

just

an island

with an

Estonian

sculptor

who

practised

Tolstoian

principles

while

he ate

raspberries

with

sour cream

the first

Mrs.

Charters

said.

But it is in the scent of wet linen in the room above

the platitudes where extenuating forest still pushes seaward.

Abolish doldrums, reveal drab ordinary soluble space.

Paraphrase skirmishes. Adhere to small bouts of raving

      sanity. Supple confiding materialism

unmask risible heroism, dream within chrysoprase

reverberations. Thorn pulls through semen's cough.

      No war without walnut's breadth,

palm frond anchors what Ontario wades.

Tessellated sill falls into the river of beginning.

Tap hydrants, forget name, bribe border guards,

      the circulation of ebony moves

chorales and archipelagos, day's ceiling too pure to wash.

Let river forsake,

let valleys rise

let provident sober

let chickweed be eaten

Lest pompous

replace grudged signal

In Vepery there is a home.

I will come she says, *undo cowardly and*

        model the beauty of his color,

the lily garlanded son. She says *I am the turbulence*

       I walk on brown petals.

Yellow-throated those also messengers

slither away. *I am kingfisher* she says. *I will world wait.*

She says *I am of red sandstone. I am the crooked way* she says.

          Yet Nabi's smashed beauty won at the fifth

and then again at the seventh gate loomed

       where effeminate meets mannerism

colludes with form and colour

Winded spear such delicate strength, *te quiero.*

You were always leaving. You arrived when you had already left.

You took down martial law proclamation posters that night Mysore rioted.

We ate ice cream, listened for vivid parakeet while flaked air settled.

Green comet fell against us.

Spread your absconding shadow.

Then and only then, infamous retreats, circuitous 12 messages

of the final days.

We travelled now apart.

You arrived at lands-end black-skirted, bare-chested, Lord Ayyappan's.

You were leaving the moment of your arrival.

Beg a public tramp upriver to touch immensity

Poke opalescent fallen bristlecone

Hundes tunge, non-profit garnet

 aubade's Zebedee enrobe shamelessness

Parse Epilogue to Ephesians

Malaprop archaeologizing Popocatépetl

20th letter a panic of *dulce.* Mock sex fuchsia

abolish Abraham, deflate cockalorum.

Eventually catch a *sentimental journey*

Roar through mineshaft, truth will wait

      Benthamite

liquor repeals Ramakrishna's musk generation

Sponge skin's vedic Irish

finger hut. Infiltrate sufferers

knowing legend's leaden sarcophagus

Smoking-skull-deer, lintel 3 temple IV

pour l'érotisme lisps the traitor

Arjuna's big picture homeland

     cleans up his debris

I'll be with you in apple blossom time.

what

rough

hand

holds

us

in

this

repose

of

vanity

Give Tulp his anatomy lesson

      In the Liberties raging

Old Father moorslept

foolfucked all over morning

changing nothing

In Oakley village, in fair,

in Bruyloft drincken by clutchthigh

bespreck seer silent stuck

Brabant netherdown as Jeroon

    swallowed then spat

out faithful

Kempish pure took he her

St Martin's white pitcher

spout-side broken

two tumble rightward

      elbows out of smocks

brown felt hat with spoon

stuck through.

Now *the slippers not the boots,*

another Reekyard to pontificate

and AH comes to sit with W's

granddaughter, festival Rhine

maiden with Bayreuth Zyclon b.

girl	**bear**	**lush**
thumbs	doorman	muddy
spoor	night	throaty
glisten	Nike	crore
crescents	leaf	frailness
stab	sap	cursor
red	moon	unhurried
red	puddle	obedience
red	dogs	pretty
dry	lamp	slides
fly	metro	invaded
away	ass	celestial
sucked	world	immerse
hour	kissed	saunters
emptied	wet	slush
	brook	
	verdant	

VII

Chupamiel.

at first two or three notes warbled

then pure ascending line unflawed

8 or 9 perfect and rising

    all the while

hummingbird perched

slight, dark, tiny, overlooking

inlet to shore, then you start

      fly away

chupamiel, silhouette to life

and another's melodic rill

above, just to the left

again another small

avalanche of song

[for Lissa].

sleek ankles,

black hair

bare-chested

red lupine spike

amidst purple

cede or seethe

as tinsel peels

away from

reluctant

teaching

plumb perfect.

Saffron gathers pert kingfisher as pinkly copperish peony falls.

Two false ceiling gentlemen and gentlewomen sub-duct

    sepulchre's large boulder to declare a rigby

at the bottom of a swell. Burrow into offal, gendered lodger.

White Mountain carnations of regulation avoid treachery

with simple premonition. Viet Cong squinch Byzantium.

Smile, child in Viking alb, pull chariot schizoid.

        Griffin chuckles.

Mr Pulls Off Petals avoids everything, titters uselessly.

Pass through prison wall, *el futuro olvidado,*

proyecto abandonado, pure Simonides.

Apple-doused buttered scythe

to timothy tremble knot

stoked reverend Mr Phillip's

    duck-billed

        cocking

nuclear little trees of spite

What last black glint glitters?

In the linden bower, on the Brecht sidewalk

    strutting, struggling

Umrika drops us

      in blights' early frown

       bolted bigoted

     hanged naked in lynch tree

o gentle Alabama,

o Whitman accused

o spring relentless

Great imperial callous forgery

      press away from

or towards that Nagasaki

tumble down philadelphic hill

    failing to learn, to mourn, to address

      your noxious march involves each

beyond all means and measures.

Defeat golden bell's

reported insult

No shame snags lost ending

No denying his girls

his toddy

his sun-burnt dalit father

In a ghost hotel

at the edge

of an ocean of unrelieved

tension, pulled red rasp

sours creamy ration

releases fleeing futures

On wing into softness

an abiding serenity

welcome dominance

balance

these romances revisited.

[to Kalaivanan].

Alder, hawthorn embower revolutionary procrastination.

Old Ireland, wise Eulalia, lower-case catholic

explain flamboyance's clover gate.

Thorns of language, Jansenism's taiga

thence Dante a hummingbird over secret meadows

Be waves not washing, his long pants taken off

See mercenaries weeping by the red water.

They resist sleep, they barter

with only chalk

    and soon after

re-appear as deer follow

Intentional iris grows, eagles

whirl Spanish letters

    javelins of

feathered jade

Thence creeps

    the English silence

between 1736 and A Preface.

    Defy the book

entertain your fellows

    After De Landa's fires

a yellow canine seeded

assertion, naked from the middle

es cadáver, es polvo, es sombra, es nada.

Antelope heart, flaked narcissus, mingled cloud and mist

All these describe his courage.

Lovely his ardor, his resentment and sorrow

his criticism of Tang rule and misrule.

Grieving over imaginary things

never to understand him

in the 10th month of the fifth year, noted

15 years after his death at 27.

What was he doing, all his combs bitter with wild honey?

Soccer does not

displease their gods.

Doe-eyed diaphanous

annals of the wind

boys will be boys.

Tuck in your shirt

Craven celibate wanting

is your name poetry?

inhabit

wilderness

suspicion

moontip

Icarus

bones

beaten

plattered

unkempt

curiosity

he fell

and he

flourished

Sparrow sun trills fearful backwards.

Abundance dirtied jilted fawn.

    Pyroclastic gentile lug cinnamon.

With 5 corinthians preening

crowd renegade never genuflections.

    Mourn taunting

deviant harmony

    grind crooked saffron.

Fickle, hitchhike, tramp away.

Black pillar of Moab

appeases sinking

    renown

Runcible roust-about

reassemble fire

    start cotton

harvest the difficult

Quickly learning

all routes away

from faded piety

    break

its stone knees

pacify its chants

warp its wails.

how to begin

washing stone

and yet

jaguar's touch

broke

constellation

where light

of cedar

in the blue

tall flame

of noon tired

while Homer

roared

washing roof

and walls

with perfect

colour

she flew

then

attacked

gave eternity

to song

heaved by

dhow back

to Romulan

urbanity

Caesars

falling

like

improvident

daisies

Whereas Plutarch's melancholy

a great heap of golden apples

beauty in Milton, walnuts

  in green rinds falling.

Hawthorne noted to swallow

a small snake a cherished sin

  drowned in honey

When the reformation

 of the world is complete to

write a dream, the real course of it

all its inconsistencies

  with nevertheless a leading

idea running through

  no such thing ever been written

    Alexander's copy

found in jeweled box, Darius', clover

still fragrant, then a monarch butterfly.

Cocklebur or Scottish thistle

a runcible barricade

lined the alley of our childhood.

Wedge-marked tablets spelled out

taxation receipts of shepherd and king.

Feathered dancers set down their adzes

  of sharpened anthracite.

Friends applaud, then turn away

to pluck silk from the eyebrows of the mistress

Near the hives on the north shore

humble and civilize sanctioned greyhound

lead him away from that mountain

to transient auburn's grander flood.

VIII

Stalwarts capture our colours.

I ask for violence

and you give

light and warmth

as your

stalwarts

capture

our colours

point to creation

as a desert

honey comb

a wasp's grey

chewed paper

home

in the

September

rafters

humming

vengeance.

Then he serves a salad
which I pronounce nick-
waaz instead of nees-waaz,
forgetting or not knowing
there is a cedilla.
It is a dessert
He says it has cherries
Pinky Madam meets the pope
in two audiences. Now Golden
Onam in Kerala. He reads Mark
after First Corinthians
Fuck me he says over and
over, then Heidegger on the
emptiness of democracy.

Wings of the bird of the heart now fled
a natural history of the soul, *a future of perpetual dark*

   Badiou notes. Larger than a quail with yellowish
ashen wings, with pleading song, consoling, lifting up,
 edible this honey-creeper. In the Baja Mixteca on
      the road to Yanhuitlán a black ant
la hormiga emplumada, came back carrying white
feather. Hence rain clouds, hence copal burnt
        like spring cumulus. Before the slaughter
all the dancers *looked like flowers* Sahagún wrote.

          [In memory of Bryant Knox].

Persian

on

horseback

all Giotto's

not to

be tamed

by clay

or art

or form

militant

silvery

soldierly

move

thence

to

taut

chaste

sternum

wave

washed

and

intended.

Pale, bum-naked

leaping creek pool

bulge modestly

grow beans, brickbats

headaches

Predictable skinny

Blinky Palermo's

pear tree blossoming

Fanny Hill poker

red Georgian livid

In Celan's

chaste briary

warmed cryptochiton

dill pentangles

Yet small camp

Buchenwald 1945.

D major fugue

to E flat major

2nd book lunar

speckled

pyroclastic gopuram

Lutheran Slavic

squiggle to

matinee sardonyx

whole truth

nothing but mourning

fourteen doors

into the courtyard

Seth testicles

cashmere withes

suppleness milky

meadowlark lightning

Arcturus gullible

impecunious Haduk

snake in the

Krestova grass

a cluster fuck.

green dragons

surround big dipper

golden crows

frost magpie pavilion

forever cautious

remain pedantic

finicky test bush

grind word

abstain from

self-satisfaction.

Lavender wild

escape Hölderlin's

variant

Ours our poverty

amorous

molasses sovereign

or wind's austerity

Tribal colours

urge

strikes over

non-payment of food

de Montaigne

deeply impressed

Bitumen unstintingly

glazes fastidious

red black sonnet

lion pelvic cruciferous

Linnaean

canto 116

Italia sinking

popes

anti-semitic

as Austria

Dirigible

abbot's

masonic ruby

Alley tawny

punk

roll over

stimulate

Achilles

Cadging

sweets

trudge

cool basalt

to trim Elijah

embarcadero viburnum

almoner's mandorla

cithern haecceity

freehold cantabile

pathic polycarp

   contumacious

appellate meng

Tell me flagrant divan

reticent

but hardly phobic

does buff battle

savvy romance?

Blotched

by doe blood

does pilgrim chassis

deliver red knotted

warbler immaculate?

Chilled

to smithereens

count out all that

remains

Request fresh

water habitat

float five

mountain towns

Red hydrangea

reduces road kill

Get messy

hyacinth talked

tender tight curlew cultivar

white to fawn indumentum

pink fading to coppery carmine

loaded with blue diamond

rhodos augustini unbeatable

with Punjabi provenance

Shaken, competitive as a river hound
take off your shoes, gulliver saliva melts bone
merriment corrupts accordion alliances
Prickled branch circulates sappy
But you proprietor lay amber grease
on fifth grade shores nicknamed argosies
as in jardyne almaund jaw jaw 's my jo

Pinks yellows leafy regal spoil marauder

White in between still textured struts on its own

Long Sapphic *new green* persists

Lyrical holds discretely a hammer of chaos

rushing to meet combination

thence blends into a tonality

impasto activism dieted down to harmonics

Stressed peat reveals schist and concentration

Walking amidst pastel, orangerie cascades left to right

a falling crystal anthem darkening kanji black

Violet angled ascending

from midway to underneath bucolic

into the hallway sporadically hued, shimmering all over

weeping à la Giverny veers off into color's lambent arsenal

and the

rubbery husband

runny as betrayal

left-handed

harebell tremor

tiger of Ceylon

sleeping

black rhino hilt

huckleberry

Aladdin

fern-headed

starry roof sieve

leans back

contests pale sky

swelling

Pard of ebony

unpietistic

wrangler of Innisfree

lean silvery archaeologist

hen of discretion

prairie sheet

of silence

laying between

rival drunken hillocks'

doe-eyed beauty

A kind of tausey mineral

eluding hammer

       ills abide

That ye love one anudder

  but leafy remain silent

Lingeringly abusive curtain

      nemesis

Mummers' mulligatawny

     unstuckery yours hisses

       alveolar cusps

weeping brown light

Dogs of love

sweet briarly

opprobrium

true as haywain

showing

contagion

of the predicate

held at bay

by jasper

lance drooling

Black root

milky white

allium grasp

stump

haul in dappled

orphaned

kame elder

deer creek's

eastern

brook trout

IX

Peonies abrupt autumn.

Walk up to

the belvedere

two steps

at a time

Tawny muscular

Apollo

now controls

these corridors

of pallor

a kind of

uterine sand

an ingestion of

peonies'

abrupt autumn

a cascade of

imponderable loss

carnivorous

ice follies

of the Duke

of Windsor

nazi pet

narcissus

temerity

boyish yet

Persephone's

campanula

round-headed

leek queen

of the night

twice names

amatory

in the rain

in the shit

in the garden

eases

impossibility

tinged with

reminiscence

flippant

docket hiccough

Hannah said a cult is what

we're talking about

they'll turn on you

you know that stuff

about shamans

well it sort

of happens there

whole villages

fired by naked

occupants

We sing

without notation

the way it

was done

before the betrayal

Kootnikoff's

bomb broken body

Trail Times front page

17 February 1962

o my poor son

oh god

my poor son

in Frank

Richardson's morgue

blown to

pieces 11 p.m. Friday

Musky prettiness

disliked being kissed

not merely

disagreeable

but uncomfortable

said scathingly

trouble is you're

too innocent

Ivor Novello

twice unbuttoned

Red Lavender

No. 11 Half Moon

trades boy

then returned

to finish his coffee

Small lusty

circumcised

Ephebe of Kritios

brown eyed

too seldom

available

practically choked

me for ten minutes

Leave your hands

in your pockets

gods and dogs

despise grand gestures

Socrates is talking

to arouse

She is a friend

rather than

his inspiration

Sit in your

high-backed armchair

refurnish

equality, nurse

wilderness

Indignantly

by riverside

sunder

purely class-based

hooded gods

of timber

in chariot linen.

Full of emptiness

bewildered by the

depth of illusion

chrysoprase persists

riddles stupidity

urinates all over

dithers

slipping

into pedant's

slow speech

syndrome

it disses fawning

fillets shush

a book

of lost music it

turns enemies

dilettantish

overripe in

britches all brass

To have lost the prize

stoked teased

arch up

against the world

right-handed

twisted, dingy

fire-hardened

When hills were

lower

goshawks

dispelled the

murk of England

Sleek buttocks

palmer's ink

in azure wheeling

traced a covenant

for archers

an inebriation

full of

Giorgione's

whispering lightning

And again
death picks
trinkets pounds
fullness nothing
Frost in all the
wrong places
summer's
zesty differential
general mayhem
marking
soft tissue
everlasting
accident
knackered
She said
each word
must be poetic
as if the
seas were milk

Bench Innisfree adept

Pea green boat

whisk us away

Pansy creased

does not glower

sprinkled melodic

intervenes

undoes

self-fluorescence.

Romp mottled

josephite nation

   purposeful

as a Poseidon

a bear stealer, apiary

contingent

and emerging.

Tired of so much youth empty out November

Deserted black-eyed Susan

paid for but was never cured by poetry

    Magpie dances on her gallows

But parakeet calls from the monumental

Catullus twice names *torrid* India

    We are full of emptiness

Bithynian wet with sticky pitch

a reminiscence of moldiness

poured to form sad seasonal endurance.

But blunt bone

boys beat

crumbles like

Roman cement

Wooden patriarch

washes away

municipal

hermetic slough

Thrush Luftwaffe

humanist

she helped

thunder storm

avenge

hypocrisy's luck

Perfumed Voltaire

harlequin

once again

leanderish and raw

Struck serrated scarred

marry dubious Anthony

Ambition a brief

shivery asylum

The vegetarian historian's

homosexual incident

in California

improved shashlik's taste

Slender agitated master

faintly screams

Protracted failure

kiting a whole country

To minister to suffering carry plump arrows

     On the large page of generosity

lure avalanche boulders

Whiff song's thyme

       raking high July azure

Sleep beneath joists of ebony

in the fort of kneeling hemlock

Write a little or a lot make
    a world with
word dust and spittle
Alpine bluebells' small
conformity though agitated
    soothes
He was roistered
    by Amazonians
hence his Irish neck broken
The leader wipes his brow
    and the women
take off their clothes
    These are abdications
So walk into the end
    of their story
with blue jadeite reminders
Is his power that apparent?

jumbled porlockian

laundromat

benjaminian

Angerlonde

alphabetery

petticoat

hopscotch

grim

tungsten

fork

deride

failure's

cloudy trousers

Like a road around a corner

never disappearing, Michigan old

glory eugenics transplanted

    became Nazi laws

Thirties' ezratics racialist

limpieza de sangre, Velázquez

awaiting ennoblement, Ezra hound

reads Italian translation, 1940

Mia Battaglia mein kleiner

stumpf, o sweet Alabama

his small light

    utterly

erased, obliterated, negated

    Hieratic Idaho's

small pebbles, turquoise

tesserae. Roman, Babylonian,

and them Assyrian archers

Ever unstill Ixion *ever turning*

<u>Re: Canto CXIII</u>

Bend coppers back to value

Rain sick burst tenor smock

Will o' wisp phospheme

Gulliver lie down underneath,

     lip Stella lower

against Balkan wars whispered

buckle snow's fragrant almond cincture

bedevil ark's timbers with literal fathoms

fingered moon tips over

      out of wordy chained yoke

beseeches crumbled Hadrian

unscroll charred pissed polyglot

heal gods

extinguish

that

sovereignty

break

his weapon

cause him

dwindle

hand

him to

his enemies

X

The Malachite Hermit.

Ocean sage settle in free moon light

Glory simple, flower-rich silks

But none desired

      Content sit

Snowy peak's fragrance purifies,

warms Jade Hall words

[To the Malachite Hermit from the Qianlong Emperor].

Crow squats on roof peak, a shush prevails.

Poet in the bughouse, St E's, O takes out ms of Pisan Cantos.

Nameless thrills we fall towards year's end crows bathing in new snow.

[The Malachite Hermit].

In summer by imperial order

tally rife virtue

As if cut out of the earth

intact, arrayed antiquity

     lift cup to drink

Disdainfully look into the distance

with nothing to say

[The Qianlong Emperor to the Malachite Hermit].

A perfect delicate simmer

barely steams away the five

aggregates, the five heaps,

        the five collections

Lu Tong Master Jade River

      wild weird words

difficult to interpret

    full of bizarre diction

none of which pleased Qianlong emperor.

[Rejoinder of the Malachite hermit].

first moistens second brandishes solitude
third withers gut's five thousand books fourth
raises sweat fifth dries bones
sixth become feathers seventh need not be drunk
chaste wind already rushing beneath

[after the Qianlong emperor].

But I am very poorly today and very stupid and hate

everybody and everything.

One lives only to make blunders,

I am going to write a little book for Murray on orchids

and today I hate them worse than everything

so farewell and in a sweet frame of mind

I am ever yours, C. Darwin.

Not feeling today or ever

or never often or sometimes like Darwin

but appreciate his tart tongue this

snow bright morning,

caught, stilled, silent

white as a mourning cat,

indelible, exhibiting its passive blanketing

it remains our friend which *followed*

with its obliterating poetry.

Crow shits white over telephone wire's cable box

Albion Moonlight goddedly disordered

Annabel and Pip just days old

    Reciting almost all of it,

struggling to remember 5th great grand child

in our kingdom by the sea

      our sepulchre by the sea

from her bed of slowly deepening dementia.

Go out to various errands

      River's arms sweep

around

hometown, heimat

      long abandoned

Mutability's flood steadied

by cordilleran stoutness

slightly eroded

      holds world

in great fluent embrace

deep time endlessly traipsing on.

Doubts refresh dusty phonemes

        embrace lineages

jive ampersands of longevity

        laws long forgotten

Emptiness reigns slow feathered

        repulses not

but attracts, comprehends

        slips into ribcage

Kuthiyottam's silver hook.

[Malachite Hermit on the poetry of the Qianlong Emperor].

unuttered, undeterred

    unread

quaffed octavians

small footed rarely

attached

    you

crumble tea leaves

drying,

        rubbed, rolled

for fortune, for prediction

crushed in your ever

silent father's palm

But not in Martin's tongue make peace

Mingle with the hounds

of spring. Moth prince

knead mackerel, battle with icons

on genocidal Christmas Island.

Hand frack maoist discordant unity misers.

Caramel-dappled count on a beautiful *elsewhere.*

   Squirming Saxon empty vulnerable Bede

defenestrate Howe's 900 species. Cellini's

black helmeted Adonis asleep

condemns moves against cardamom rift.

Curried escarpment seeks

      abyss of sleek ankles.

All is forgotten, sonnet-sweetened lad.

Cropped sure circle back brightly kissed.

Shuddering three days

blood floods

despite quick lime

　　Orders from Berlin

cooled with buttermilk

soothed with sucked mints

　　　single bullet,

cartridges litter *sein und zeit*

　　　small hands reach out

from a thousand bleeding pits

[In the Polish forest].

Nocturne's ninth

coils up *what is poetry*

Byzant's posthumous?

Silenced ruby emperor

      massacres?

Where Kali tutors?

Voluptuous

Sophia Circumstance?

Or propriety of river

pew, distraction's beauty,

joven Bamyan tender,

tinder or tungsten,

redundant as crow's stupa?

At the Ministry of Rites

intoxicated, drinking

chrysanthemum wine

wash ink-stone

    try new brushes:

Wild river paired sky

Yellow glows daylight

Gull and heron

unaware of each other

Hermit asks who are companions?

We unroll scrolls together.

[Qianlong Emperor to himself].

Tongue sharp dusty blue
      Sleeking dialect muted
hum cunning vellum's dose
smooth rounded squealing
   Dun days then
hounded by flyby exorcists
    Put on suit of jade,
walk into the fire.

But repeatedly walked

      sea-naïve

despite dangerous fires in London,

chariot amber,

      the little fall of comets

Sharpen thorny prod

Banish the four thousand

The dead exiled silence zero.

Query quantum tart canto

Ah so! pour wheat piss prandial

Noisy door sent here assures

Fresh in me plant eyrie days

Harried curse lalala caboozer

Without speech sign up for pennies

tip over loss lenders

    Sinning limits mead crescents

Hail more allergy gypsies vaguely.

Alkibiades an averter squandered her treasury.

On balsam steppe rigorous Avakum arbitrates

Psalm alters clover flow

At 10 minutes to seven a reservoir of coriander

dreams without concepts.

Swaddled castigate regimental grin

where water defines dwelling and demise.

Sashaying sharpens abundance

amplifies amaranth, Memling dizziness well protected.

Cupped boys tup

unadorned

sleek boxers

Rain breathing

rumpled thighs

Preened

in stupor's

iris corral

daft dandelion

spits umbeliferous.

seamless, truculent, revolutionary,

river's concretion an isthmus, a tartness,

Blake next to Defoe, Cromwell, Bunyan

all without sleepy underarms

of cathedral, *nothing can add*

beauty to light,

at swift's sharp call rain takes off its clothes.

red cinnamon flowers

pink orchids

as in peach

and plum poem

shining

Book of Self

watchful

never worried

never deprived

emerald

emperor wrote.

[Qianlong].

XI

Bag cherry kisses.

Green moon hooked by

silver chain

death slipped down

spiked with lady's foil

his children bandits

bag cherry kisses

Walnut's lunar gall

balked four times

insisting he

did not know

pear tree's loss

hid clutched in

liberal bosom plaintive

Who would tell us anything?

Pomegranate soap from weeping

Italy?

Who sings curried

seven sister porridge?

Cat's cream?

Who indents uranium

exploded over

a city of wooden houses?

Who rides charcoal horse now?

against stern dreamy azure

        with heroes

sandaled or in the

battle between the animals

excited bodies acting out in marble

tickled little rollick

    cinnamon

to silent room's digestion

devoid of orthodox regulation

bottom's daffodil picked

    consoling sky

asleep and raining

Fiddle proudly even when set against better.

    Leaking spread the chiffon of small poems.

2 larks larking have not stabilized anything yet.

Cast solid in silver, blue lotus

    son of Ptah shake your sistrum.

Nefertem bend over creation a rarity ever faithful,

rain-weltered, unhurried, generously released.

Slender to an earth postponed

as the sea says its own Mahabharata

moonlit Shiva ashes in our ink

Eradicator and producer

      open those little

countries where ice and blue flame

reduce us to trembling acacia's song.

Meet them with sand

dripping from parchment

sleeves

Jealous sycamore

brave shale's disclosure

Gorgeous torero,

Couperin's light-fingered star clatter

communist of the green-chain

ever yet in paradise.

Come to the healing sands

lounge a hundred years as

wanton dynasts squabble

Let go, lift dolmen

carve that music

paint mahadevis dancing

Browning tanager

marigolds at your door

Euripidean in accuracy

Giotto's howling angel

What was the word

for ruby in Malayalam

he asked?

He undressed

Pretty, almond-eyed, a

waiter in blue briefs

addressed need effortlessly

All was in tune

a gold thread over

our shoulders

Little palm of Jordan

teak wakened prick

in a circle of lantern light

cocoa oil and jasmine

melting splash

of arduous honey

Parse obligation

melt sweetness to its origin

Like a letter from Engels

disputing the weight

of corn and wheat

imported from Carthage

mark the decline of a

mode of production

What fluctuates? The

difficulty made

by small acts

of corruption?

To oppose, to gild

to blaspheme, to indulge

to re-enchant

to re-spell the obvious

Shush. Be quiet.

Naked idealists, pacifists with gelignite

protesting world at war the historian

bombed the lion on the left.

In the spiritual apple orchards of the

Sect of the Naked sectarian debt increased

There was no relief.

Cedar oil rubbed on your face

that you be not weary

What comes out of him?

What causes joy?

Fly up eldest one,

stand at the ladder

pure westerner

axe belongs to heaven.

What is beneficial?

Lingering never get home till after supper

Moor the womb

Over the river, over the water of truth

    cold unforgiving chrysoprase

Going forth by night, going forth by day

do not be taken doubled lion orders.

Erase the secret of shape

      Knife of broken bones

soldiers are javelins

Report to the empty ones

      the walkers

the citizens of the city of the bee

Eat in every pleasant room

     Doubled lion is glad

Do not drink urine at the lake of flames

      Nefertem, I am the man

I know your name, I am one with you.

Not derision fussy old mole

despite a sea portaged

saffron intimacies

desire's useful tadpoles

    nor death forgetting

hallucinated October

Speak slowly to avow

the dispossessed, the enslaved

      Bet against

propriety, tears, sighs

all difficult efforts pity complains of

Encumber sieve with a river

Solidify reasonable with swank

Do not ever promise June

Never say *withdraw tamely*

Winter crosses over late

and unconvinced

then attempts to purify

colt handsomely

Jam him jay to

invertebrate

All for the emancipation

of the obscure.

Mudlarking in the failure of the divine memory

    cuneiform tablets wash ashore

Heroes taxes land measured

crops owed gods gone

Ailerons assembled

take on one black sea per day

With entropy lieutenant aboard

love his ledgers

As if pretending to need

sweetened surplus

eye sudden famines.

Sully orb ill piano sybil

navigate away unanimously

Strike ruffled ocean

    Rich in trembling song

distill fast disappearing forevers

Mute return to gentle publics

Advocate wry chords, precipitate

reconnaissance nosedives

    as brown earth

knees words' Homeric pride.

materialist legends

supporting spring

meant to be bodies

visions trellises

verses and reverses

else purgatory

foxily re-enters.

Quickly repossess core colours

furious Hannibal hisses

      Poach words worthy

Sea senses love initiates the world

the opal cutlery of the sky

      With oiled lenses greasy

speculate without a trace of indulgence

Wait secure at the door of dawn

      at the window of rainbow's stalker

defy fury, sunset's standstill.

Behind every monarch

a mountain in Michoacán

XII

Linnaeus named you messenger.

Theophrastus remarked through handshakes

poor orchid unites. All prefer you

Linnaeus named you messenger

Red hot mamma, code red, iris fulva, bronzy Valentino

toreador pants down, tongues

    out, sepals undone

sparkles chartreuse yet purple defines.

with Persian

circumcision

yellow punk t-shirt

Silenus

alleged but

more likely

a car

exploding

students

proliferating with

Kalashnikovs

civitas dei

a medieval

ventriloquism

robots satanic wallmarts

      fixed by sent money

filial sunlight

piles up songbirds

nuclear imams

Georgia crackers

New England sharpies

ineradicable fantasy

pushed ever westward

to bees' desert salt flats.

Love does not require your wind of Chelsea amber

Instead please make us laugh.

Who is loved among the Romans?

Grime or cornucopia?

Who falls asleep on sarcophagus' lintel

Who leads two lions to the wedding of Ariadne?

In chalcedony Eros holding a large black butterfly?

Demuth's sailors pissing?

Apparitions improvise to question our arguments

and silence recollection but instead

stun hallow's harvest

All violence, conscience eaten

in schematic surges

sleeps in the office of the deity

      Like a statue fragged

all lovelies fall down

Alert September upbraids

   unmarked indignant purities

in quietness scourges light impaired.

Upholstered *philosophes*

pencil outlines

of the peach

Freckled volcanic

humanity

wretched

with flowers, fruit

syllabic parfait

Narrow waist

broad shoulders

solid silver nocturne

Nefertem attends

waits, advances

embraces

bends over creation

with all of his own.

[For Rajeev].

Wars, convoys, battles, deaths

necessary victories

spill on the linen of capture

Survive the quince of his anger

With pollution removed

incoherent we are whole

hawk-high hunt

Dwelling however uncertainly

deluded at best

that which fell, still falls

we remain good stewards

in high abstract colour

Foolishness lends

wolfish Aprille

spring's dorsal

Scrupulous

unconscious

inutile

hangover's

frankish

oblique

plaything

a duration

of owls

Walk amber

river as Pleiades

    fall

never forgetting

Pale light then wine

on the Amarna shore

The liars will not wait

Softened voices well

-loved in

rhythm pajamas

relaxed by gentle

performance, well

behaved carnations

suppers

grapes wet with

promised cleft

Healthy ever ready

cross into this

dusty teeming world.

I have seen the beasts

vociferous milky divine elephants

cocky crusty sweet sheep reciting the fabulous as

birds convulse in deeper skies

Drink from auburn asters

valved, testicular, laugh.

mentioned

in Hindemith

Mallarmé's

white-outs

by Haydn's

prussic angels

in Scarlatti's

melancholy thence

vast endless

chattery

a meadow

an offramp

a parsed

interrogatory

   abidingly

lovely dwindles.

All is youngest errs quickest

Blooming sassy horticultural

soggy gassy sect itched

knocked endless

Eminent artiste selved

    tick tock speaking

Why merely so immersed

as sibling and kindred?

Ere hope sprang must plot line

    lash and last?

You a ditcher? You a dictator?

      Yes mister

see singed meistersinger

voguing lithe spectrums.

Sleep in quaint sufficient penitentiary

Chew glee occipital

Do not reverse sere omega

Search for monstrously arch white swan

Plebeian nervous demon and nearly wolf

      sentry guarantees the scaffold

Ragnarok folly airmails ill to dust colleges

Tell me circular histories

      Quelled, defeated, cheap word

glamming tantalizes these adventures.

Poem's sweet misery

affronts the monster

who distracted yet remains

    still treasured

Cruelly me I abandon his

Let us attend to lances

still lifes, and surely whoppers

Unstop golden cruet

Purslane again approves

architecture's uncertainty.

Think each cadence queerly

when things, persons, events

remain servants, natural

chrysoprase tablets

sometimes elemental corrections

to monarchic interiors

            Las Meninas an example

Proceed like a poet with selected music

             in a botch of rhythms

Toads and lizards work out

world's passing modernity

Each private soul empties

       into the commons with humility

That sea, tidal, endless, deepest, despotic

remains directed to the same or similar

observes sober creator, our enduring Nefertem.

Delight risked is a pine

Rose is a'bloomin

Kirsch is a tear

Sports between birds

dominate

Rupert's Land

is water without

end

Death muddles

universal

a lie book of

fathering grammar

This remains the first law.

A bowl of Egyptian irises

stone-carved dates, plums

and corroded coconuts

Among utopian syllables

tangles of spring

      Wither from here?

Fall into yellow calyx

    of the red tulip

Rifle tomb's treasure.

Break the Door of False Endings

Prune apricot so that it blossom

XIII

We defeated him.

Appled jesus never disappointed her.

Counter with a tasty *bon-bon*.

We defeated him, the Ontario reverend father.

> We certainly knew.

Franciscan torturers, executioners and executions.

Yeats' reviling their surplices and birettas.

Prismatic Euripides

false Alexander

Alkibiades the vaunter

loses Sicily

Socratic gentle

impasto vocalise

streeted

endless river

Cursive running

script carnelian

tremble skies' empire

of unfettered blue.

He is a lord of cunning, his mother does not

    know him or his name

The bug of heaven ate their guts

He who is at the willows

      on the north-side of heaven

broods with kettles cooking thighs of his eldest

Older than the old he smashed vertebrae

      He has eaten the red crown

he has swallowed the green crown

He feeds on the lungs of the wise

Shadows are taken away

      from those to whom they belong

He is that which dawns, which endures

    His favorite place *among the living*

in this land, forever and forever.

[after a pyramid text].

Very near lost myself

in first daylight

I go down to take crabs

it was very thick fogging

Walk down mile tide

come back I try go home

I colden fin no way

I walk round 2 hours

    I have hear

small Black crow speaking

So I go where he speaks

He found small Creek

Now I follow the creek

an I get up the house

4 hour walk round

thick fog all day

[23 July 1907]

Set Okeanos in a walnut shell

and Queen Mab's atomies, magnates

fulsome steak eaters

will slouch away underneath tart lemony frogs

Caramel boys' reproductive

duties set momentarily aside

an indisputable beauty, a vast nothing

of ritual refreshment taken and lost

Good times pacify hens and garrulous

      nurses

Thrones and dominations, a vast elysian

emptiness, crumble

Haven wreck reef death's insult

   Slow murmuring priestly embalmers

from the green side of the

river humming reassemble corpse

inflated, wrapped, salted, extended

   The other side sere unto foothills

Lotus prince gobbled by

crocodile god, the cat-headed stone of

silence Nefertem will not redeem

Shard fantasies correctly

Ancient miners bring copper from

Danube hills, occupy Gibraltar refuge

Soft territoriality distracts calcium depletion

Courage never golden treaties

Blue rose's cruelty or silence's cinnamon

he danced and he pleased

lilac listens lightly

locks luck

chrysanthemum careful

coronation charismatic carries

daffodil dancer, danger

demands devotion

tulip thralling tongue to text

shapely as Dante's

home-calling apple tree

diagnostic cryptic

allen key

resubmit

tender called

white teeth

in Manila smiled

snowing horses

of responsibility

with Ethiop voracious

at the window

They came from where brown-eyed susans grew

traded in copper, dietary prohibitions and ganzies of jade green

They were like me and you, but independent and not necessarily

fragile. They wore Bedouin clothing of bright colors

with tulip skin underneath, of varying shades of reddy ginger

      or an idle cyanotic blue

They were creatures of carbon and joined at

various times of the festival calendar

with others who pursued similar but complimentary

ventures. Trespassers with a purpose

          they fanned out across

the inhospitable lands of the great Khan's interloper state.

Dusted forget-me-nots knot sky jeans-blue.

Long alpine fields, whiskey jacks, magenta vertical spruce cones

a sparseness herbaceous and floral, mingle. Its stillness

not the pall expected, but the silence

at the core of the imagined world of the heart's singular

community of doubt and hope's traction.

You ask that we guard each other's small breathings.

Many more you wish us and I begin to comply

chatter on as a crow, who that day troubled the

lost Samoyed, whose name was Sky.

[for Bob Melnick].

Blow up reddened grave's

venery of asses

Impulsive plotted testicular

this testimonial

disperses junkets

to heirs and poets

putains and smiths

Across these lactose

foundations

faked congruence

depresses light

Non-bridal exchange culture

an emic of taut grief

disguised as flecks

to the world-historical

a dose of London streets

yore to orrery.

Late uncle alcoholic godfather

stumbles down dark

hallway in the *dom*

almost falls into regal coffin

where lay withered

psychotic broken nerve

touretted perfectly obscene

rebarbative shivering

Truth a slow knife

ambient ankle of

violent peppermint

    evacuee

clenched wet and sulfurous

through his slowing hair

Ganga falls to pool

unselfconsciously

he drinks

poison

his neck is

blue he is

dusty with

cremation ash

thoughts orphans

glitter

because he

coniferous

and resolute

as a moving

continent says so

[after Cuntaram].

kouros of San Blas

lightly haired calves

feet bare

ripened *ritornello*

helado natural

Juanito joven

Janitzio Uruapenensis

    a moon a sun

a hummingbird

ground honey

    rudding

castellated

black waiter pants

unbuckled

Cedar roots stitched-up rip in

yellow freighter canoe

Brebuf's letters and Dale

Carnegie read aloud through

whose advice Renata

jam was got for

campfire-roasted bisquick

And self-heal's purple spike

and pearly everlastings around

straw-hat's brim

where Hope in the Twenties

skated miles home

What is in apparence a lake

but is the narrow interior lake

or the *lake at the centre*

or the *lake of*

being's beginning

In late March rain,

ides long passed,

kanji roaring

pluck nourishment

well-runnelled

angled against

chimerical falter

Turmeric dilution

monger

Elysian disproportion

calculate willowy

saturnal fireman

    without

Lascaux umlaut

Dresden flames never

extinguished

that land of chives

tiger lilies

sidereal monkeys

mesoliths of

river-dislodged

damp granite

smelted copper

gob smacked

heroin boys

horsing

summer roads

geraniums inevitable

young sequoias

never allowing

relaxation

chuffy carnelian

aglow

on the eleventh page vague shadow below white singlet

short-haired brush cut, providential enduring silence

      dark lord of the 5 rivers

or mine own Nefertem, narcotic, heliotropic

monkshood small corrective draught

dream recital of the *jungle inside.*

Like Popeye's Sweet Pea

Goon Show's *kiss me Eddie*

        tantrum scholar

in that short hallway

in cast off chrysalis

of swaddling clothes

pulls out Kandinsky colours

    of infinite

contraction and expansion.

XIV

Stops the stench of the world.

which is at the nose

stops stench of the world

who is perfect

in being or not being

standing on a lion

with two plumes two

necklaces virile

['Nefertem'].

but poisons, of the blue throat

weapons of blue

and those hyacinths known as blue dicks

sacrificial blue

   and the words:

[brine] [thwart] [heir] [tithe] [banshee]

will be vertebrae in a

poem yet to find the morning of its writing,

Nothing built from top down

as if that were apparent

in those days where

hay was stooked

cedar barns built to shelter

ochre horses of dawn

We produced little

are nothing and

remain in the outskirts

This plaster city

once upon a hill

surrounded by

lakes of aboriginal

blood and

the enslavement

of Africa.

Dank islanders flibbertigibbets stone away

Sailors who sleep off golden fleece searches

also launder purpose-built history

    where it was all lost or gained

Leprechaun who produced Brecht

from party missal dissolved

    in a panacea of glazed crazes

as Le Maitre put lions capable

of devouring us into his thick grass

Wake up Endymion, horse of Selene needs bridling

      Corsair rebukes meek river's

daughters. Moon-distressed studies work

to hide temple walls

      So delphinium whose Acropolis

whose bareback, whose broken empire with violets?

Your ambitious tea cup

           answers *grams of dust*. Start again at the

drunkenness of Noah, red chalk on paper

      Leering son or handsome calf to Pon's waterfather

husbanding animals till dove, rainbow

and Ararat. Stallions in wave crash, that foam delirium's.

garter snakes

in rows of

unpicked beans the

visiting

disappointments

of related adults

uncle of

the Spanish flu

soon mourned by

rainbows

kokanee

freshly caught us

who came

as a cloud

a shower

a ring of bitumen

a lost brother

on the

other side

of the river

that lilac that gingko

chamomile with lavender

    that Friday golden

uncurled

oldest one in the windows

     of the sky who

hears enemies fall through his

fingers.

speckle

refiner's fire

jubilant

tamarind

epigrammatic

shivers

Masaccio's

    neophyte

Mallarmé ripples

ochre

hand prints

coastal come

by chance

    arcadian

refurnished

silent as

snow falling

Andenken, fir leaf or bear tongue

sharply pleated Alberta

Lowland sand blown

all over azure canyon

Fleshy dusty bugler

heralds blue Cochise

Timberline dreams talus

slope's two pronged

     instability

deadly yet contained

Larch bowing with pride

on mountain bashful

     sharply

needles caliph to attend

dark venus penstemon

With mercy

abide fierce children

Hide liquor in the

house of colour

upon colour

Churlishly this

un-transfigured night

orders *Brasil desde*

los ríos sacerdotales

to memory.

Afterword: Shard Refusal

Recarving the Chrysoprase Bowl is, in McGauley's words "Tuned by lateness" ("In river" 80). It is a life's work, begun in another time, in the making for almost half a century, and only now nearing its completion. The origins of the impulse to begin it go back to some of McGauley's earliest and most formative experiences in Castlegar, B.C., in the early 1960s. The name *Recarving the Chrysoprase Bowl* was first used as the title of a booklet, 32 pages in all, printed by a fugitive publisher in Vancouver, Black Stone Press, in 1979. A few years later, and McGauley had several poems published in successive issues of Gerry Gilbert's *British Columbia Monthly*. Anyone active in the underground world of Vancouver's poetry scene at the time might have expected to see his name more often as time passed. But the opposite was to happen instead. A pattern takes shape that holds true from the mid-1980s to the present. Experience seems to have indicated to McGauley that recessivity is poetry's calling card, and its making, a work of withholding, leaving out, and taking back. *Recarving the Chrysoprase Bowl* becomes the name of an action responsible for more than the booklet with this name on its cover. Repetition of the artisanship of carving suggests the continuance of poetic making in behind the scenes and set changes of literary culture in British Columbia in the 1990s and 2000s. McGauley was intensely and publicly active in many fields: electoral politics, trades unionism, participatory governance, local history, and cultural activism. An obsessive traveler, he was in Mexico, the United Kingdom, Ireland, Taiwan, Spain, and the Philippines, as a young man, and at age 50 left for the first of nine long trips to India, the latest in 2019. Now and then, one may catch indications that he was writing poetry all along, since the end of the 1980s. But what little he published scarcely hints at all that was underway. Only now is the scope and breadth of McGauley's work in poetry visible in published form.

The activity, re-carving, is consolidated, now, in a printed artefact, this book, that constitutes the first of an anticipated quartet. To follow is a second, subtitled "In river never ending", forthcoming from Galleon Books. A third currently bears the subtitle "COME HERE

LONE SOLDIER", and the fourth, "What is Given".[1] The sequence in its entirety, *Recarving the Chrysoprase Bowl*, then, is still in the making at the moment of writing. One might then wonder if an afterword is appropriate for a project that is not finished. Is this not to foreclose on possible changes of direction in a sequence that suspends its ending in the name of future changes? The purpose of this afterword is not synopsis and closure but a furtherance of what McGauley calls "Shard refusal" ("In river" 208): measures to guard the sequence from opacity and disconnectedness, and yet preserve its refractory disunity intact. "You shard refusal", a voice protests in a recent poem, taking its cue from another in the second, forthcoming book: "Shard refusal, refulgence a dialect of the unanswerable" ("In river" 208). That which is "sharded" is not crushed or in shambles: "Morning sharded tangles classical to retain autonomy" ("In river" 116). *Recarving the Chrysoprase Bowl* is a work of poems in sequence, each with its morning that is neither poised in apartness, nor self-entangled in the verbal undergrowth of the others. The sequence is cumulative, building up its images, landscapes, names, sites, and settings, one at a time. Though there is no plot to follow, there is a dense fabric of reiterated language-actions and verbal patterns to take in and move through, whether one reads deeply, for motifs and allusions, or for the surface effects in which the poetry has its profoundest life: its rhythms, sound-textures, derangements of syntax, and acoustic concretions. The most repeatedly invoked of all the entities in *Recarving the Chrysoprase Bowl* is none other than its protagonist, or the closest there is, in it, to a protagonist: neither a person, nor a thing, but an action, the flow of the Columbia River to its confluence with the Kootenay, and to the whorls and spinning dishes that the fluid mechanics of opposing currents carve, and incessantly re-carve, into the maelstrom of this confluence. The colour of the water taken up into this whirlpool is chrysoprase, a cloudy whitish green that is both flamboyant and understated, luminous and obscure. Not the shard, then, but the shared language-action, multiply-reiterated, kinetic and connective, is the compositional principle active in *Recarving the Chrysoprase Bowl*. A commentary that identifies some of the undercurrents, arguments and references that many of the poems share may serve, then, in the role of a provisional, if not conclusive, afterword.

---

[1] In what follows I also refer to a superseded rough draft of this fourth book that McGauley had called "In the auburn bed of righteous adventure".

1. "Here beginning returned to, only memory can go forward"

A précis of McGauley's life as a young man calls to mind the venerable formula *ora et labora*. On one hand he was steeped in the devotional culture of an intensely Roman Catholic household and the religious community associated with it. But the trappings of a life in the bosom of the church were woven into a working-class life pattern on the cusp of a new epoch in the history of British Columbia. There is every indication that the centre of gravity of his household was not religion, but work. Before he was a teenager he had a paper route: in high school he worked fire and security duty on night shifts at the sprawling Celgar sawmill in Castlegar, and in the summer, stationed at a weigh-scale for logging trucks hauling in and out of the interior, McGauley was in the deep woods, near Nakusp. His father was a smelter worker at the Cominco installation in Trail, where he and his brother, Jim McGauley, would also work in time and where, in the local idiom, it was routine to be leaded, i.e., found to have elevated levels of the lead in the bloodstream. Celgar and Cominco are but two firms associated with the accelerated program of resource development implemented in British Columbia in the 1960s. The effluvia produced on the banks of the Columbia may have fed into the soundscape of McGauley's poetry: "Socket turners smelt copper, seething lava trilling all the while cooling" ("Auburn bed" 144). A cryptic salute to this industry's marriage to the river is in the last book of the sequence: "In the beginning dislike of green binaries was then followed by the smelting of lead, zinc, gold, and silver" ("What is Given 45). This patching of the first words of Genesis, "In the beginning", onto the catalogue of metals hints at the overlay of opposed forces, clerical and commercial, spiritual and industrial, that works unpredictable effects at the depths of his mature poetry.

A pulp paperback that has left neither its title nor its author in his memory hit him, nonetheless, with a memorable rush of self-awareness: "Peru is where it all began as a child, the exit from piety into history" ("In river" 139). This was but a children's book about a Peruvian mummy, yet veiled with dark scrims of meaning. By an unlikely stroke of fortune McGauley, probably looking at random for books about South America, then chanced to fall in with the chronicle of the old conquistador, Bernal Díaz del Castillo, *The True History of the Conquest of New Spain*, nightbook of "Tenochtitlan's *noche triste* [sic]." This, he writes, was (in his mature reckoning), or should have been, "A night religion ended its hold" on the human mind ("In river" 204). Reading about it was a turning-point: "Incurable teller old teacher Bernal Díaz del Castillo plaits self-managed midnights" ("In river" 136). He who plaits is binding up the lineage of the present that McGauley felt he was living in from that moment on, though the consequences were not clear to him for years to come.

In *Recarving the Chrysoprase Bowl*, passage from the stasis of piety to the movement of history is associated with a specific waterway, the Columbia River. In the fourth book of *Recarving the Chrysoprase Bowl*, McGauley writes that he was "born in Columbary flood year" ("COME HERE" 93). That he was born just then seems to mean to him that before, things were placid and peaceful. Into this harmony of the human and the natural roared the floodwaters of 1948 and then, later, those of a manmade, successor inundation:

> It was, it were earlier, it was before the first, it was bluer, trailing 10 commands. But river ran over valley-wide, over movie marquee, about the drowned downtown, over bank striding snowmelt. Hydrologic posterity repositioning sublime subordinate. Splashed shins, washed school boys and girls, carried silt to skirl foreshore's delayed peonies. Smelter workers escaping 10-acre farms melt rock, endow mercantile slap-shot ergonomic ("In river" 61).

The force of waterpower that had been "sublime" in the natural world is stilled through the engineering of large dams and made "subordinate". The world-ending flood of 1948 recedes and begets its inglorious "Hydrologic posterity", the personnel of B.C. Hydro, who were to preside over a second, managed flooding of some of the same areas, later. If this sounds like a bathetic reduction performed on the action of an archaic creation epic, McGauley is aware of the events retold by Eileen Delehanty Pearkes in *A River Captured: The Columbia River Treaty and Catastrophic Change*. The neutrality of the word "repositioning" begins to lift the curtain on a history of official indifference to the lands and lifeways of the Sinixt people, revisited later in the sequence. The human and environmental costs of promethean land-sculpting projects lie, then, in the background of *Recarving the Chrysoprase Bowl*.

That the Columbia is an international river may then implicate the fusion of times and places in McGauley's representations of it. The regimes of de-inhabitation and displacement that precede the rearing of so-called megadams link otherwise distant worlds.[2] In the dreamscape of *Recarving the Chrysoprase Bowl* the specter of Burt Herridge, MP, tireless opponent of the Columbia River Project, materializes just long enough "to rhyme Cauvery with Columbia" ("In river" 97). The damming of the Kaveri river, travelled by McGauley on one of his sojourns in India, is hotly disputed by the neighboring states of Karnataka and Tamil Nadu. It is as though the transborder politics of dam construction tears open a perspective from which borders recede before vertiginous analogies. After McGauley dates his birth to the "Columbary flood year" he veers from his own natal shores to "the native place | of Namalvar", Tamil Nadu:

> born in Columbary flood year
> now how many times to the native place of
> Namalvar seeking to return and those arms
> and heart otherwise just joe
> blow in the moon house of the construction ("COME HERE" 93).

The name of the Hindu saint-poet Nammāḻvār means, according to A. K. Ramanujan, "our own āḻvār." An "'āḻvār' is '[one] immersed in god", and "the root verb āḻ means 'to immerse, to dive, to sink, to be lowered, to be deep'" (ix-xi) . To his authorship is ascribed a vast sacred poem, *Hymns for the Drowning*. Though *Recarving the Chrysoprase Bowl* is no hymnbook the purpose of some of the poems in it seems to be to memorialize drowned or drowning parts of the past. One could claim that there is more than one "drowned downtown" in McGauley's poetry: an ensemble of clustered references to specific historical *topoi* stand in its depths like the remains of submerged plazas or once-peopled meeting places. What, then, are some of these lifeworlds?

McGauley is known as a scholar of British Columbia's Doukhobor community. Dissenting, protestant, egalitarian, and stridently iconoclastic, the Doukhobors were and are a Russian Christian sect with

---

[2] On the Columbia River Project see Wilson 2019, and on the socio-political consequences of large dam construction more generally, Murphy 2011 and Nixon 2010.

origins that lie in the 17ᵗʰ century. "By 1895" writes one of his associates, Greg Cran, "they were practising vegetarians and their pacifist tenets had led them to a complete break with the military." This breakage took the form of bonfires on which were hurled state-issued weapons of war: "By burning all their firearms they dramatically demonstrated their refusal to kill" (6). At the turn of the century, with financial support from Leo Tolstoy and Tolstoyans, Doukhobors migrated in the thousands from Russia to central Canada and then to the interior of British Columbia. But the place presented in Doukhobor folklore as a haven and a promised land proved fraught with snares of its own. Utopian, separatist, and acetic, the Doukhobors wished to live fully apart from the state and its institutions. Measures to safeguard this apartness took the form of the spectacular acts of negation that were to secure the notoriety of the Doukhobors in the public imagination for years to come: incendiarism and nakedness, the destruction of material wealth with fire and the discarding of clothing in demonstrations. Both, Woodcock and Avakumovic record, were practiced by Doukhobors in Canada as early as 1902 (176-181, 197). This time of unrest was quelled momentarily under the leadership of P. V., Verigin, known to his people as Peter the Lordly. It is he who moved to settle the fertile wedge of land between the Kootenay and Columbia Rivers that he then named Brilliant, a naming that McGauley mentions in several poems. When Verigin was assassinated in a railway bombing in October of 1924, some Doukhobors blamed the Canadian government, while others pinned the deed on extreme factions of their own community. In British Columbia, feuds over his legacy were to escalate. The Orthodox Doukhobors, in communal villages at Pass Creek, Brilliant and on the Ootischenie flats, were targeted by the Sons of Freedom, on raids from Krestova. The violent internecine feuding that belongs to the recent history of this community enters the first book of *Recarving the Chrysoprase Bowl* early, and remains in it to stay:

> Confluent inter-penetrating valleys
> to higher mountain villages
> houses burning by the
> hundred, glacial terraces
> stagger up Zion ridge,

explosion

and his death lift train car roof

Village and river

pine and sawmills, highways and

pilgrimages, spring floods

and funerals

birthdays and twilight woman

carved from a stump

her sculptor rowing out

to save children from drowning.

Intoxicated orchard, lip of childhood

where patriarch hills

reach beyond villages on

the Plain of Consolation (14).

McGauley writes of the fires he had seen one night from "Hope's land", both his aunt Hope's property and, figuratively, from a standpoint of high hopefulness. It is in this spirit that, according to a letter to Fred Makortoff, he began his studies of Doukhobor history in the 1970s. He had, in his words, "a romantic notion that the Doukhobors were a persecuted people, struggling against harsh governmental instruments of repression both in Russia and Canada." In McGauley's poem the Columbia River Basin becomes a natural amphitheater in which this dramatically hopeful history of protest is seen again, as though reperformed. But later, as he writes to Makortoff, "in the late 70's my views changed. I no longer understood things in a black and white fashion. Economic struggles for wealth and power by a small layer of the Doukhobors became more apparent" ("Letter to Makortoff" 3). The closing reference to "the Plain of Consolation" nonetheless associates the name of this settlement – in anglicized Russian, Ootischenia – with the consolations of demystification and freedom from unfounded hopes.

Long before Verigin's subagents secured property rights to the place he was to call Brilliant, this wedge of land was known to the Sinixt by the name of *Qepi'tles,* or *kp'itl'els* (Pryce 153). It is lost to time what this multiply spelled word or words meant, exactly, to the many generations of the language community that once lived, worked, and buried its dead there. One of the poems in *Recarving the Chrysoprase Bowl* is dedicated "In memory of Alexander Christian, Sinixt", the last of his people to work the land before his expropriation by Doukhobor newcomers. While the poem's first sentence sounds like something from an outdoorsman's diary, the second takes up a wider history: "We continued up lake amidst shrill mountain sides, elevations of impenetrable forest, within a home of creeks with cutthroat. Lead, zinc, silver brought capital's will to organize and rule" ("In river" 206). It may be that the sound of the place-name *kp'itl'els* is supposed to be there, obliterated or under erasure, in the words "capital's will." Christian, Sinixt, had petitioned for years to have his property recognized in law, only to see it purchased out from under him in a land transaction between a private owner's estate and Verigin's organization (Pryce 62-69; Woodcock and Avakumovic 226). It is he and his family who "disappeared to territories downriver. Whose graves were ploughed under. Whose land, utensils and possessions [were] stolen, fenced in, who could only by boat come up from the river to their bit of homeland" ("In river" 206). Brilliant prospered, then declined, its last remaining structures brought down by fire on the night McGauley memorializes.

This site, *kp'itl'els* and Brilliant, is a major vector of meaning in *Recarving the Chrysoprase Bowl*. It is the nearest place on land to the confluence of the two rivers, the Columbia and the Kootenay. Seen from Castlegar this is, in his words, "the other-side of the river" ("In river" 117), not simply the other side, but the *other-side*: a far shore and a place apart in both space and time. This otherness is a vortex and a confluence-form that draws in what would not normally be found together. Where the two rivers meet the whorls and eddies that McGauley names in the singular as the chrysoprase bowl form in the water. The torsions and fluctuations of opposed currents carve and re-carve wobbling cones and spirals in the flow of the river. This is a place that nature seems to have predestined for meetings and cultural confluences in the human world. But this is also where newcomers and long-time landholders, exiled and colonized, Doukhobors and Sinixt, were cast as antagonists in a conflict all but scripted in advance by a sequence of opportunistically mismanaged land transactions. This tortured history overdetermined the conditions of the possibility of meeting, undercutting what could have happened, had others been in effect instead.

Offshore to the west and south of the place Verigin called Brilliant there is a small island, once owned by a Russo-Estonian émigré named Alexander Feodorovitch Zuckerberg (1880-1961). On this island he erected his house, resembling a chapel, which incorporates elements of rural Russian church architecture into its design (Charters 26-28). He built, then, at the confluence, where McGauley's poetry also sets its foundations and finds its grounds. A poem near the end of *Recarving the Chrysoprase Bowl* describes him as a "secular anchorite." His name, cut apart and translated as "sugar mountain", is placed next to the words "bitter" and "sour" ("Auburn bed" 136). He is a man with an appetite for opposites, "raspberries | with sour cream" (122). On his island he is both in exile and at home. Technician and artist, gregarious and secluded, his tenseness and gentleness make him, McGauley suggests, both ghostlike and futural:

> In a ghost hotel
>   at the edge
> of an ocean of unrelieved
> tension, pulled red rasp
>   sours creamy ration
> releases fleeing futures (139).

The memory of his craftsmanship is represented in McGauley's poetry as a zest for antagonisms and high contrasts. Zuckerberg, non-Doukhobor, was nonetheless "Tolstoian" (122), and his way of life was, McGauley recalls, acetic but not religious. Local knowledge holds that his "Chapel House", as it is now called (Charters 26), is modeled after a country chapel in a famous painting by Isaac Levitan, *Over Eternal Peace*. McGauley's Zuckerberg works, less with beams, planks, cement, or bricks, than with tensions and countercurrents. His hermitage, both secular and spiritual, intensifies and reconciles the tensions worked into its construction.

    The cultural geography of *Recarving the Chrysoprase Bowl* is, then, multidimensional. References to Castlegar and its environs jostle with namings of sites in India, Mexico, America, and Europe. The transcontinental and overseas transit of mineral and forest products out of the interior of British Columbia to innumerable export destinations may be one enabling condition of this orientation to space. But McGauley's Columbia River Basin is a multiplanar composite topography where memory and the imagination supervene on the real and literal. "Zion ridge" (14), in the mythos of the Doukhobors, is visible on the rugged sides of Mount Sentinel. Peru and the Andes, in the active imagination of a precocious child, might lie hid behind its upper heights. To substantiate, unravel, and reconstitute such intuitions and misprisions would take arduous wayfinding and a long tutelage in the medium of poetry. It is to the work of McGauley's first writerly associates, mentors, and companions that we now must turn.

2. In Search of the Local

It may be the voice of Fred Wah that intones, in McGauley's italics, "*nothing in nature is made from* [the] *top down*" ("In river" 170). The italicization both holds this utterance at a distance and also imparts immediacy, nearness, and force to it. One of McGauley's friends at Selkirk College, he had come from the tutelage of Charles Olson at SUNY Buffalo and that of Robert Creeley at the University of Albuquerque. Wah was a mediator of the New American Poetry in what must have seemed at the time an unlikely outpost of its influence, deep in the Kootenays. From Selkirk McGauley took his transfer credits to Simon Fraser University in Vancouver, where he studied with the poet Robin Blaser, and also the scholar of Olson, Ralph Maud. Robert Duncan came to SFU in 1971 to do a reading, and in the student newspaper, *The Peak*,[3] McGauley measured his poetry against Olson's example and found it wanting: "Give me Gloucester, Idaho, or Castlegar", he pleads, anything but Duncan's theatrics. McGauley skewers the poet he had seen in the spotlight: "Robert Duncan: the Poet as Actor. Robert Duncan: the Poet as Pinball Machine, with 185 different lights." Something was missing: "there is an emptiness of a long line breaking without PLACE, tether or focus." Place, he seems to define as what is vividly felt with the senses. He instances *The Maximus Poems*: "There was Olson, poking around, asking in bars, pulling in fish nets, he knew the stiff breeze" ("or, the Going-On").

When Jeremy Prynne came to Simon Fraser to do a lecture on

---

[3] McGauley's writeup was published under the title "or 'The Going-On'" in *The Peak*, 17 Feb, 1971, on p. 17. That summer, with Brian Fawcett and John Scoggan, he also interviewed Edward Dorn for *The Peak* at the York Street Commune in Kitsilano. This interview is reprinted in Dorn 2012, pp. 14-29.

The Maximus Poems IV, V, VI, Maud enlisted McGauley to record and transcribe it. This transcription was published in *Serious Iron* (a special issue of *Iron* magazine) in October of 1971. In the same issue McGauley published a poem in prose called "<u>DEER PARK</u>", about a paradisal waterscape on the Upper Arrow Lake. This is nothing if not a poem of "PLACE": it is a transcript of vividly felt experiences, relived in memory.

> There, then, <u>the lake</u>, a suspension, mindless, no thought: sense rises like heat waves. The unity of rock, river bed, mountain and lake, water . . . a motorboat its lazy sluice dissects the suspension. The parts fall into the whole, my eyes blink. The water is cold at my feet, the sand hot and sticky.

A tangle of sensations, tactile, visual, and pre-verbal, stills time and sets the mind at rest, until the stasis of immediacy breaks, and what had once been whole breaks into the dichotomy of hot and cold, sand and water. In *The Peak*, McGauley had censured Duncan as follows: "He is not LOCATED, but in the cabals of symbols, untethered myth and pinball sound schemas." A countermovement to this overinvolvement in mere sound takes place in the prose-scape of "<u>DEER PARK</u>", which ends with an epiphany of the here and now, its speaker "Lost without thought, but <u>located</u> in this moment." But there is no mistaking that this locality is one of the haunts and idylls of his childhood, hence continuous with other imaginative borderlands and neighborhoods of memory. This obvious fact troubles the emphasis he gives to being "<u>located</u>." What then is at stake in the magnifications of this word, the underscoring and the spelling of it in capital letters? Or, put different, what is the emphatic concept of being located?

A poem he wrote in 1974, "DOMNA", takes to the language of liturgy to negotiate the local overlay of cultures. Through the maker of frescos, Giotto, McGauley apostrophizes a syncretic Marian figure:

> Giotto this day   give
> us the   angels
> who   announce
> who   bear   the
> news   of the
> flowering of

her womb
Mary Madonna
of   granite
Provencal [sic] Domna
Anastasia Holubova
and
found in the peasants [sic]
cloak,   Guadalupe
or in a primeval
cave, Fatima
and Bernadette
Souberous [sic]: or
of Savignano
bear me
      the worlds son
      chryso tom
      rainbow warder
      trickster   pilgrim (Maud, *Divine Comedy* 9).

The tensions deepen as the names accumulate, and the "chryso tom" who speaks here seems conscious of deserving the epithet *chrysostomos*, golden-mouthed, with its pejorative implication of honeyed blitheness. Not only a move beyond the literal and the physical, then, but also new ways and means of organizing the field of speech and sound in the poem would have to be derived from elsewhere, or devised anew.

McGauley can be seen on the cover of *Serious Iron* with the rest of its inner coterie of contributors. Visible on the wall behind him is (according to editor Brian Fawcett) a "map of North Central British Columbia circa 1818 – stolen from the SFU library's copy of Daniel William [sic] Harmon's Diaries" (6). The map is there to say (presumably) that the objective of *Iron* is by no means to reach as many readers as it can, but to be true to the local life of a chosen place, in this case not the coast, but the interior of British Columbia. *Iron*, Fawcett states, was a contradiction, affirming the local but possessed with the poetic language of writers who were not locals, but outspokenly American. Its core of contributors, everyone there in the room on the cover of *Serious Iron*, were all under the influence of one man, Charles Olson. His example was felt as an injunction to go local, to forsake the global and generic, to forge communal links to a specific place of abode and to be there, fully and emphatically.

Ralph Maud, too, was inspired by Olson when he launched an ambitious audiovisual project in the summer of 1974. His objective was to shoot a film that he eventually called *The Divine Comedy in Castlegar B.C.* The leading role in this production belongs to his student, McGauley. The following synopsis is printed on a handout distributed at its première in 1975:

> Tom McGauley, formerly a student at Simon Fraser University, has returned to his home town in the Kootenays, working as a postman and experiencing the landscape as a poet. Through Tom's friend, seventy-eight year old George Padowinikoff, we get a glimpse of Doukhobor history, which is so much a part of the life of Castlegar (Program).

From coastal Vancouver, Maud's student moves inland to Castlegar, and enters into the life of its local history. His film seems to position McGauley as a living example of Olson's ideas going into action. What, then, happens in *The Divine Comedy in Castlegar B.C.*?

In one scene the camera follows McGauley on his bicycle onto the humble Robson Ferry, plying its way over the Columbia River. He dismounts and Maud films him in the middle of answering a question about the recent past. A crisis of disorientation had overtaken him at SFU, though he leaves the details unsaid. He had, in some way, attempted to combine the incompatible: a soberly alert life, disabused of illusions and attuned to reality, and the "beatific poetic stuff", intoxicating and mesmerizing, dished up by his enthusiastic expatriate teachers, Blaser and Maud. A dichotomy emerges between foggy Vancouver and the sunlit interior. Asked by someone (probably Maud) behind the camera why "we come here", McGauley answers:

> It's away from the fog. Apples grow here. Douglas Fir and Ponderosa Pine is here. And the mountains are here, and there are people – there's a community, and a river runs through it, and people work and live, and do it – and die as quick, like that woman who hanged herself in the City Centre Motel. Van Gough [sic] painted a picture called "The suicide's house", and I'll show you the

suicide's house, except it's burnt down. And it burnt down, boy, it burnt down. There's nothing left. That's why I said to you before: if the wind blows the wrong way it'll kill you (Maud, *Divine Comedy* 7).

The word "here" resounds like an affirmation but this resonance comes down to its regular repetition. The liveliness of McGauley's extemporized monologuing becomes a focus of interest in its own right. It is as though the rhythmed patterning of his utterances were a counternarrative opposed to the message that Maud's film seems intent on communicating: that what coastal megacities like Vancouver withhold, the truth of the local, the hinterlands reveal. On the contrary, the rhythmic fluency of McGauley's words seems to say: the secret of the local is not stability but motion, not security but exposure. Here the quick and the dead shake hands at a place in which people "live, and do it – and die as quick" as the wind changes direction.

In an opening montage of old photos, a moving album, McGauley, arms folded, leans against a car. Beside him is a man who had lost his life before the film was made, Robert Donaldson Craig, or Scotty, long-time friend. In a scene shot across from the enormous Celgar installation on the far bank of the river McGauley pores over the details of his death:

> He just went to a wedding and decided to come back to Castlegar in the middle of the night, a beautiful beautiful drive, probably very drunk, and the car went off the road and the steering wheel came down and crushed his chest and killed him. He fell down Pass Creek Falls, he went through motor cycle accidents, he had nine lives and it was finally up to that one and that was it. So I can't feel bad. It was a tremendous shock that he got what he got (Maud, *Divine Comedy* 11).

The local, then, far from a bedrock of stable being, would be the locus of turbulent, foreshortened becomings. At its most intransigently memorable and abiding the local is umbilically linked to that which is evanescent and exposed to every contingency, from minor mischances and contretemps to life-ending accidents. McGauley's friend's death suggests, then, the fading of the illusory stability that attaches to the local and the emergence of wider horizons beyond it.

This shift in focus from the scene of the local as a literal place to a convergence of multiple times and places is arguably the point at which *Recarving the Chrysoprase Bowl* begins. The very first poem in the first book is an elegy "*In memory of Robert Donaldson Craig*" that bears the dateline "26 sept LXXII" (v). This elegy revokes the singularity of his individual identity and disperses the vestiges of it in a field of other names and plural pronouns, as though committing his ashes to the elements and mourning the dead at large and as one:

> Who know nothing
> no reward for them it reads
> these have all perished
> loves jealousies memory passed out of
> nor will they ever play in whatever
> is done under the sun (v).

McGauley's threnody, in "DOMNA", had sutured together its catalogue of names into a long apostrophe modeled on a Marian litany. In an inversion of this strategy, the subject of his dedicatory elegy is first compared to one sacred counterpart, and then another. He is both Tammuz, and also kin to Hades, pursuer of Persephone:

> and the girls wail   him
> Tammuz   gone
> he would have said yes to her
> did and is dead
> Ishtar bring back this man
>
> a substance around
> yew a cloud of light
> how does it fight now
> how holds he that axe
> how pursues he now Persephone sharing (2).

In class with Blaser, McGauley says in an interview, he had honed a faculty of responsiveness to "a world heartbeat of poetry" (Interview 10), somatic in its immediacy and universal in its historical range. That McGauley was to follow his intuitions of this transcultural heartbeat into the southern hemisphere is predicted by a handmade broadside of his elegy he had printed in a small edition. To the left of the poem a row of Mayan hieroglyphs about the cycle of the seasons and the taking in of the harvest acts as a visual counterpart to the verbal listing of fertility figures such as Persephone and Tammuz. The generative scatterings of Robert Donaldson Craig's remains spring up, later in the sequence, in oblique references to a phantom "captain" ("In river" 85), a guide associated with the idea of carrying escape plans into action, and moving from a world founded on false hopes to one in which a good death may be hoped for.

3. Arguing Atheism

A good many of the poems in *Recarving the Chrysoprase Bowl* are in foreshortened lines of only a few words apiece. A case in point is the following, from the first book (the one you now have in hand):

> That *was* coming
> to be our *is*,
> optimum flatness
> roundness
> reaching, willing
> what binds
> the place to others
> lost you
> somewhere
> on Citlaltépetl (12).

In Mexico, McGauley was to envision a particular *was* that he took to be the abiding condition of what *is* in the present as he knew it. He sketches the parameters of this *was* in an untitled essay about his poetics, published in *West Coast Line* in 1990. "For myself" consciousness of "the darkness of our time" means, in his words, "attempting to become conscious of a North American dimension to this darkness which originates in 1519 with the conquest of Mexico Tenochtitlan" (Statement 137). It is not easy to tell who or what is "reaching" and "willing" in the poem that mentions the mountain, Citlaltépetl (Pico de Orizaba).[4] Is the "*was*" of line one, steadily becoming "our is", to be identified with the "optimum flatness" of line three? This "flatness" could not be the "roundness" of the next line, or could it? There is a drift in the syntax of this poem that both compounds together and screens out possible doers of the two actions in its fourth line: "reaching, willing". This occlusion of agency resembles the "darkness" of McGauley's essay to the degree that it too does not conceal anything in its nightscape. As though the volutes and inclines of the real mountain were reduced to notational geometricizations, a "flatness" here and a "roundness" there, placelessness subsides into a hemispheric "North American dimension". But spiriting away this place's every particular does not reveal that which "binds | the place to others". Instead, this bond recedes, "somewhere | on Citlaltépetl", in the form of a "you" that seems to vanish in the distance. It is as though "our *is*" can only look on as its inseparable counterpart, "That *was*", absconds deeper into the lands of the conquest.

In a later poem that also refers to Mexico there is, instead of a distant "you", an "ourselves", coupled in the plural:

> Magnificat
> podzolic
> susurration
> exultate
> 9 morpheme
> Shadow
> -infolded
> motley
> the Dance
> of the Old Men
> ourselves
> huaraches
> slapping (32).

---

[4] In Mexico City there is a traffic circle (and slip roads to and from it) named after the mountain. McGauley mentions this area in a poem with no title, published in same issue of *West Coast Line* as his essay on poetics: "I remember Frida Kahlo's house and the Zapotec spoken and the earthquake fissure in the lobby of his Citlaltépetl apartment near the Parca México" ("She said it was anger" 56).

The Magnificat is named but not used to bind non sequiturs into the same form of song or poem. It is but the polysyllabic overture to a poem that patters answering rhythmic *sequelae* to its measure. The recherché words accumulate, "infolded", in a "motley" that is not mere helter-skelter verbal patchwork but a particular kind of performance, modeled on "the Dance | of the Old Men", an important event on the festival calendar in parts of Mexico. It is the faintly obscene "slapping" of the feet of the dancers in sandals, "huaraches", that this poem's "ourselves" constitutes its tentative identity around. The "Old Men", feet a-patter in the hot-footed up-and-down steps of this dance are "Old", not in the sense of exclusive seniority, but that of the old age that comes to all in time (or to all those spared premature life-endings), "ourselves" included. It is hard to evade the suggestion that there are corporeal determinants of experience that bind "*is*" to "*was*", past to present, even (perhaps) "exultate" to "9 morpheme", or "podzolic" to "susurration".

Bodily ills and the sorrows of age, McGauley seems to say, may be an archive: if not a trove of documents in hard print, then a record of cause and consequence. A malady and its cure often surface together in his poetry, as in "Alder treats dog bites", or "Juniper *scopulorum, of the mountains,* a wash against fever" ("In river" 135, 117). Herbarium entry notations record treatments: "Ephedra for wakefulness"; "monkshood disciplines arrhythmia" ("In river" 137, 127). Seldom do autobiographical disclosures slip through, but they sometimes do: "Pain flares then abates or becomes a constant, a normal, a reminder of the fall and concussion. And the tremor, familial, inherited" ("In river" 174). The mnemonics of pain and aging enter into McGauley's thinking about his own writing. On the last page of his essay in *West Coast Line* he writes of poetry as though it were a patient in a clinic, suffering from a "pre-existing condition": only, in his words, "the pre-existing condition is darkness". On one side, he thinks poetry is endangered by a worldwide "culture industry" (137); on the other by a public mood of gloom, inertia, and indifference, what he calls, early in this first book, the "melancholy | following from Guatemala" and by implication from all the lands of South America (11). His "old teacher", the memoirist Del Castillo, is "incurable" ("In river" 136), a sick man regurgitating his tale. But the illness metaphor also applies to poetry in McGauley's diagnosis of its condition. It is as though poetic language as he knows it is seeded in its very fiber by material-imaginative residues of the conquest and its aftermath.

In a poem that sounds autobiographical, McGauley's "I" says: "Conquistadors were the first part of the cure from religion" ("In river" 195). This simple statement is tinted with irony. The conquistadors could "cure" him of his piety for only one reason. It could not last once he knew the whole story about the incurably lethal epidemic diseases they had taken to shore with them unawares. Early on, in the first book of *Recarving the Chrysoprase Bowl*, he quotes the same Latin verses that Cortez once had to brief his king about the Aztec Empire's vulnerability. "*Omne regnum in se ipsum divisum desolabitur*" or, as McGauley translates, "every kingdom divided | against itself falls to Smallpox Virgin" (9). The words "Smallpox Virgin" (besides the cult of the Blessed Virgin) call to mind the rampant spread of so-called virgin-soil epidemics in populations unprotected by inherited immunity. "Founding mulchers", then, in his words, "brought smallpox divinity to map a continental childhood" ("In river" 97). The same words are to return: "*smallpox divinity* remaps continental childhoods" ("COME HERE" 19), his own included. In the family home was a photo of Eugenio Pacelli, Pius XII, enthroned on the *sedia gestatorum*, or, as McGauley puts it, "12 pox coeli borne on sedan chair in our childhood" ("Auburn bed" 47). "If only", he groans, "gods stayed in their places and did not molest with epidemics of smallpox, measles, influenza." McGauley links his atheism, then, with what he came to know about "Spanish new world [sic] smallpox epidemics" ("In river" 124, 146).

One of the poems in this book of *Recarving the Chrysoprase Bowl* is based on a work of anthropology by T. F. McIlwraith, *The Bella Coola Indians*. In it he describes the movements of a supernatural being that "can travel only on fixed paths" (48). Anyone unlucky enough to camp in its way, reports McIlwraith, is visited by fatal hemorrhages and wastes away from loss of blood. A story follows of a man who survives the visitation of this being and becomes a shaman, though without the power to heal others (556-557). McGauley re-renders and selectively rewrites this story as follows:

But in his dream a strange animal and minutes later
    at the fire his nose bled.
No one could stop it. Friends assembled one burnt his nose.
Was he alive, scar still visible. His mother wept, he asked her to stop.

They had slept in the path of swaiaswax, *who travels on fixed routes.*
He lay in darkness, suffered in sunlight.
Inside his head he heard a bee, words of his song brought to him.
She spoke his name. He shook his hands as if to dance (22).

A condition of this poem's making is its suppression or occlusion of its immediate source, McIlwraith's book. But then, the many iterations of this book exist at a distance from its own primary sources, McIlwraith's informants. A poet who freely samples from a work of ethnography risks compounding the abstraction of ethnography's prising tale from teller, the story from its inner cultural mediations.[5] Still, McGauley's positioning of his poem about the creature, "*swaiaswax*", is anything but abstractly dislocated from purposive mediations. It is, instead, determined by surrounding references to the raging of smallpox in both hemispheres of the Americas. McGauley seems to interpret this story as a mythological inflection of an indigenous response to European epidemics. The fearsomeness of the being that travels on exclusively fixed ways would then suggest an imaginative projection of the unstoppable spread of new illnesses. This interpretation is itself a projection, in need of its own critical unraveling. Still, McGauley's attentiveness to contagious illness and continent-wide epidemics suggests an empirical and practical orientation: his is a citational poetic that seeks, not to detach myth from its material origins, but to sift the mythological in search of the historical.

The chrysoprase bowl is a figure of motion under arrest, of time held still, if only in the imagination. A sense of what this looks like can be found in one of the poems in the first book. It is the source of the fifth section's title, "Eternity Craved and Thwarted":

> Torrent's silt of longing,
>   rice terrace rising, winnow of alder, breeze
>   of dismissal,

---

[5] In Nuxálk oral culture, suggests McIlwraith's editor, John Barker, a storyteller not only tells, but also owns, what is told, the tale. The telling, too, is undertaken, not just anywhere, but in a context that determines the conditions of its transmissibility. It is not told, then, so much as entrusted, transitively, to a hearing (xix-xxiv).

all sharpen adze's dumbed morning

Littered with cardamon or mint
be it wave-ripped or firmly furious against
decay marbleized, the impossible,
        bowels to liver
stain love's lost nape, crow's proudest
        flight away from
    into pinkish resemblance
of eternity craved and thwarted (89).

This is a fictitious eternity, then, but still active and at large in the world, both "craved and thwarted" by those under its spell. The words "decay marbleized" and "pinkish resemblance" may call to mind pink marble statuary or the illusion of breathing life into stone, of giving impermanent life a form as lasting as stone. This would be the very "impossible" that the title of the first section of the first book, "Flense Scriptural from Impossible", imagines in its apartness from the words of sacred scripture. But here, McGauley seems to give up on this wishfulness as the signature maneuver of the religious consciousness. The river of time is merciless, but its torrent yields a "silt of longing" that takes on alluringly different forms in history.

In Egyptian material culture, McGauley finds the basic paradigm of which his childhood religion is but one particular instance. He labels Egypt "that evading kingdom of the classic pretended escape from death. Into endless dynasties, tomb texts, embalmers, natron and tar, golden masks and watchers in ebony" ("COME HERE" 11). The first part of the sequence (that in which this afterword is printed) is named *The Book of Gates,* after a tomb text that teaches its readers what to expect in the hereafter, and what to say to each of its many gatekeepers. The petitioner must halt at every threshold and say the name of the one who watches over it. That royal tombs were in or under pyramids may have made him think about pyramid schemes and other forms of "fraud" such as the manufacture and sale of fake antiquities: "Settled blue dust of millennium crusts over as pharaohs divulge death not defeated. But the golden masks last. Fraud transhistorical pyramid texts make clear." It is no secret that, in his words, "death shall have all dominion": both "the great and grumbling dead" lie "all solid in silent nothingness" ("COME HERE" 121). But the avoidance of this nothingness seems, from his perspective, to link forms of religious life that lie worlds apart, ancient Egyptian and modern Christian.

The Nile River, writes McGauley, in a poem (from this volume) that borrows from Herodotus, both "befriends" and also "abolishes" the "impossible":

> There a river interminable, bending
> along the Libyan plain where it shouldn't
> abolishes, befriends impossible, flows on forever (29).

A priesthood safeguards the secrets of its annual rise and fall. But the river is, McGauley writes, not only "templed", but also "commercial":

> There a river from a desert, nonetheless fluid, broad-banked,
> templed, commercial, full of vegetarian silt. In its
> attendant monuments bulls tick-free sacrificed,
> un-tasted supple menhirs, black to tail
> > fertile as a Nubian smelter (29).

A real or imaginary traffic in coils of copper incites an associative glide into the field of acoustic technology. When McGauley writes that "Here speech begins within copper wires" he seems to be thinking about copper voice coils in amplifiers. A speech that is alive all along its cupreous transmission coils begins, McGauley says, not in expressions of affiliation, but of "desertion":

> Speech begins in desertion, detains absence
> slaked such that distribution off stage
> rakes charred bones of victors.
> > With tendril tenderness
> speech seizes cold chaos where all surges (29).

The Nile's harmonizing of opposites, fluency and aridity, desert sands and fecund mud, is a model of a speech that "seizes" with "tenderness". What is seized is, presumably that very "impossible" that usually finds expression in the "scriptural" alone.

McGauley's going back to Egypt seems driven, in part, by a recuperative counter-divinization: to reclaim the Nile's fantastical desert origins for the imagination in its worldly profaneness. That this river, in his words, "befriends impossible", makes him try to imagine its friend, the impossible, as a face with a name. He finds this name in *Love Poems of Ancient Egypt*, co-translated (from Italian renderings of the original hieroglyphs) by Ezra Pound and Noel Stock. Instead of the Pharaoh, the Nile's consort is "Nefertem, sweet pal, new born blue lotus, set out for the god of the handsome face, he who will not come up from the river". He is both, in McGauley's words, "mine own Nefertem" and also "our enduring Nefertem" ("In river" 201, 19, 159). The Nefertem-composite seems to be a *figura* of the intersubjective and transpersonal energy supposedly imprisoned in the scriptural and extinguished by it. If the life of this energy is contradiction, then the impossible, rid of its sacramental husk, might be identified by McGauley with the transformations of this being and others that resemble it.

Still, fires of spiritual zeal may be lit by having done with scripture. Here we need only turn to McGauley's own research on the history of the Doukhobors of British Columbia. In Russia the Doukhobors were, writes Aylmer Maude, "an illiterate folk, who seldom put their thoughts on paper" (5). This unwillingness was part of an anti-ecclesiastical devotional culture. Doukhobor worship begins in negation: no scripture, no priests. The further to the margins recede the trappings of textual culture, the more central music and psalm-singing become. This body of psalms, woven from "orally transmitted doctrine", is known by the name of "the Living Book" (Woodcock and Avakumovic 25). The origin myth of this name calls to mind the riparian poetics of *Recarving the Chrysoprase Bowl*. Legend has it that the first Doukhobor was a hermit, Danilo Filippov, who, after intensive study of the Bible and the Russian Orthodox liturgy, threw both into the Volga. In verse he is said to have praised "the golden book, *the living book*", sung and not read, known, not once and for all as a body of codified teachings, but in the fluidity of its many iterations:

> The corpus of psalms and hymns was called "The Living Book", since it was constantly growing and changing according to the experiences of the sect, in contrast to the Bible, which represented in Doukhobor eyes the frozen wisdom of a past age (Woodcock and Avakumovic 25, 26, 22).

This "growing and changing" calls to mind McGauley's incessantly revised river book, or books plural, *Recarving the Chrysoprase Bowl.* There is, then, an affinity of his poetics, and his field of scholarly specialization, Doukhobor culture. In one sequence of *The Divine Comedy in Castlegar B.C.*, McGauley sits next to his elderly friend, George Padowinikoff, carver of the kitchen implements called Doukhobor spoons. On film the old man sings a funeral elegy and tells the tale of the emigration of his people from Russia. The name of *Recarving the Chrysoprase Bowl* calls to mind Padowinikoff's woodcarving and one of the poems in it cites the very words that he says on screen. We must, then, consider McGauley's thinking about the Doukhobors in greater detail.

4. Iconoclasm and the Doukhobors

A poem in the second book of *Recarving the Chrysoprase Bowl* revisits the genesis and persecution of the Doukhobors in late imperial Russia: "Czarist dinosaur absolute with outlays of state revenge, oppression and Siberian exile" ("In river" 186). To evade the vengeful spiritual partner of the autocracy, the Russian Orthodox Church, Doukhobors dissembled, temporized, or kept silent. Woodcock and Avakumovic, writing in the aftermath of arsons and bombings, insert a caveat about this historical practice of secrecy. Doukhobors accused of "evasiveness regarding their own affairs" are reliving "a heritage of the deviousness that life under the tsars made a necessary self-protective device" (13). McGauley keeps the memory of this history of persecution alive in *Recarving the Chrysoprase Bowl*:

> o children of Tolstoy's paid passage by the SS Lake Huron seethe in devout radical rejection of the Book, the Priesthood, our first real martyrs brought into the bosom of Mt Sentinel and river's chrysoprase confluence, my father fishing its eddies. Martyrs remembering, *Vechnaya Pamyat*, in *memory eternal* ("What is Given" 25).

He takes up, then, with the Doukhobor *ethos* of rejecting many-tiered spiritual authority. This "radical rejection of the Book, the Priesthood" is a catalyst of energetic negativity that he seems to want to nurture and maintain in the historical memory of his poetry.

Conversely, the very motto "*Vechnaya Pamyat*, in *memory eternal*" is scorned in another poem. An unnamed writer uses it to avoid the real truth about the Doukhobors: "But of course she makes *Vechnaya Pamyat*, Eternal Memory, stand within and against a discourse of property and national identity" ("What is Given" 25). Countervailing testimony can be heard early in the sequence, in this book:

> Hannah said a cult is what
> we're talking about
> they'll turn on you
> you know the stuff
> about shamans
> well it sort
> of happens there (175)

The "there" is not so much one single place as a multiplicity of places. It is the site or the ensemble of context-parameters in which a familiar pattern of action plays out. The abolition of spiritual authority turns over into its opposite, "theocratic despotism". Rid of its externality, the written word, as the inner voice, is immediately the voice of a particular individual. Though "in theory", write Woodcock and Avakumovic, "the sect rejects all authority", in practice it conforms "to the direction of spiritual-temporal rulers whose authority is almost dictatorial" (29, 22). The further and still further splintering of cult leadership is the subject of many of McGauley's poems in *Recarving the Chrysoprase Bowl*. Tolstoy's protégé, P.V. Verigin, dies in a blast of dynamite, and his people's communal solidarity dies with him:

> lordly Peter blasted
> christic peasant
> sectarian squabbling
> universal brudderhooded
> failure those orchards
> that blown up boy
> that pile of flesh ("COME HERE" 44).

The "blown up boy", is Harry Kootnikoff, obsessively remembered in *Recarving the Chrysoprase Bowl*. A bombing raid ordered by one of his people's latest ascendant insiders had gone wrong, and the explosive detonated in front him. McGauley's poems to Kootnikoff are serrated, set in short lines, nakedly ridged:

> Kootnikoff's
> bomb broken body
> Trail Times front page
> 17 February 1962
> o my poor son
> oh god
> in Frank
> Richardson's morgue
> blown to
> pieces 11 p.m. Friday (175).

Instead of "Eternal Memory" it is the violent dismembering of Kootnikoff that McGauley's poems report and memorialize. In a later poem the syllable *off* seems to wrench its muffled sound free from the words that contain it: "Kootnikoff off to bomb something, a school or post office it was said. Against this broader campaign of *terror in the name of god*, rewards offered in post office wanted posters."[6] It is the nature of cultic power, he thinks, to shatter and splinter, to multiply, instead of settling, sectarian recriminations.

Suffice to say, then, that he had a major research interest in the enticements and dislocations of cult leadership. That he had this expertise means that he is interestingly positioned in the history of the New American Poetry. In later phases of its life this literary movement furled or folded over in a way that overlaps with what McGauley had seen in its worst form in the Kootenays. It is instructive to consult the last section of the last chapter of an influential book that the literary critic Robert Van Hallberg published in 1978. He is the first to make a distinction now taken widely for granted by many readers of the poetry of Charles Olson. This is a bifurcation of his poetry into starkly separate segments that each correspond to a different authorial persona. The

---

[6] "In river" 186. McGauley is silently citing the name of Simma Holt's *Terror in the Name of God: The Story of the Sons of Freedom Doukhobors*, which dramatically narrates the events leading up to Kootnikoff's death in its first chapter, "Born to Terror" (pp. 1-6).

Olson associated with Black Mountain College is a politically active, civic-minded, would-be teacher of his people, who, leading a retreat to the mountains of North Carolina, had moved to the cultural forefront of his times. But then, this is not the only Olson. There is also the isolated yet captivating outsider who was to win over the minority culture of a later time. This is the poet that Van Hallberg calls "Olson in the Sixties" (40). Who was he?

> The *Black Mountain Review* never became a national journal, but in the sixties, beginning with the publication of Donald Allen's anthology *The New American Poetry* (1960), Olson gained a national reputation. During that decade he became a cult-figure, consulted like an oracle by young poets and little magazines [...] American literary culture appears to have no way of handling a poet like Olson, committed to a pedagogical and rhetorical poetics, short of labeling him a shaman, and Olson perhaps had no experience at rejecting what was, after all, flattery (215-216).

This sketch of an ambitious poet's regressive ego-identification with vatic archetypes, shamanic, oracular, visionary, or demiurgic, might apply, with but few modifications, to Robert Duncan, or even Robert Creeley, among Olson's generation, and to Robin Blaser, John Wieners, and Allen Ginsberg (among others), in the next. McGauley, a scholar of in-cult behavior and social mania, ferociously critical of the cult leaders of the Doukhobors, writes poetry that often reads, very much, like that of the later Olson, syncretic, notational, oracular, and seemingly, saturated with private and privative meanings. What to make of this resemblance?

It is from inside of Selkirk College's hilltop library that the speaker of McGauley's very early poem "DOMNA" looks out and loops together, in the plural, the many semblances of the same beatific figure. Witness a later poem in which he resurveys the site of the same campus lookoff but in a very different voice and mood:

> We revisit that early college mysterium, an imported scree slope, granite turned into adamant non-miltonic flows of later revived skepticism, with roots in Voltaire, the great old man sculpted by Houdon, the everlanding undoer of all the reliquaries of the *E at Delphi* ("What is Given" 68).

Fred Wah is part of this verbal picture of times past, if only through the title of his thirty-year compendium of collected poems, *Scree*. In cancelled lines from a rewritten draft, McGauley looks back to "That *then* when the one known as *False Master Falls* argued, *nothing in nature is built from top down*". But this master's voice speaks from the "*top down*" to the lower plateau where its tones position the listening ears of its disciples. It is as though the very curvature of the landscape were to correspond to the telltale modulations of a voice that belongs, not to any one person, but to many, then and since. Active in this aural memory is the thought of a miniature speech genre in which the magian poet, "consulted like an oracle" (as Van Hallberg puts it) dispenses wisdom from on high. In retrospect, McGauley seems to say, induction into this "mysterium" disabused him of the trust he might have once placed in the authority of such oracles, and in the mantic word-games that support it.

What, then, about Robin Blaser's cenacle at Simon Fraser University? In the third book of *Recarving the Chrysoprase Bowl* he is elegized as a "great teacher" but also a bad historian, beholden to a false image of the past: "In the bright pastoral lapses of judgment mister crystal balls loots melancholy without shifting gears." Blaser practiced crystal-gazing and owned a crystal ball. In his vision, McGauley seems to say, history is crystalline: deceptively transparent, falsely luminous, and above all, fragile, weakly vulnerable to recalcitrant facts that threaten to splinter it. "The red-breasted holy forest man", writes McGauley, "needed reminding by a handsome student with a Gandharan moustache, that obviously slavery did exist at the core of the poet's golden dream of Athens and Sparta" ("COME HERE" 80, 10). The *ethos* of this interjection is important to *Recarving the Chrysoprase Bowl*: McGauley's Blaser omits or forgets cruel details that this sequence's self-assigned remit is to recover and foreground.

To the example of Blaser's poetry, McGauley opposes the tutelage of a very different kind of teacher. Porter Myron Chaffee (1900-1989) was a labor activist and a former writer for the Works Progress Administration who later emigrated to the Kootenays, where he befriended McGauley. "Porter and Robin were", he remembers, "the best of mentors", companion antitypes in polar apartness ("Quick Notes" 6). Both had significant attachments to California, and to the esoteric. McGauley's "bio-obit", as he calls it, to Chaffee opens abruptly, as follows: "Leaving bars with poetic recitals, dialect sugars newsreel, Chanticleer calls against all wars" ("COME HERE" 48). Chaffee's ricocheting displacements land him in the wilderness of the forests of British Columbia. McGauley's Blaser, conversely, seems to live in a voluntary inner exile from a disenchanted outer world. He is the author of *The Holy Forest*, the title he used, starting in 1993, for his collected poems. This name is seized, inverted, and pulverized, several times, in McGauley's poetry. It is the "holy undone forest", as though denatured, fully and wholly, into its opposite, not a refuge but a desert ("In river" 186). The worldly spirits of Chaffee's life and activism disclose another view of the forests of the interior. "Dreary pan smacker dredges | locust forest pine beetles rampage" writes McGauley in this book (82). That which is on the rampage, at large, in the forests is a socio-natural infestation, the human-caused population explosion of the mountain pine beetle. The name of the city of Castlegar echoes in McGauley's sarcastic reproof to the ownership of its local pulp empire: "Castigate algae-covered rocks in the pulp mill polluted Columbary, you great overseas barons of forests to chopsticks" ("Auburn bed" 144). The forest, then, is wholly undone, not so much a holy arbor as a mine for the invaluable plasm, pulp.

McGauley's agonistic closeness to Blaser led him back to his teacher's modernist forebears, not only Charles Olson, but both Ezra Pound and, arguably, T.S. Eliot. One poem bears witness to the political ecology of the interior of British Columbia: "naked hills hold shivering poplars | acacia traces jade protest against smelter smoke" ("What is Given" 100). Cominco and its smelting works on the Columbia deforested vast tracts of land. The Federation of British Columbia Naturalists (BC Nature) recount the history of efforts to repair the damage:

> Black Locust (*Robinia pseudoacacia*) trees were introduced to the Trail B.C. area to stabilize steep banks that had been denuded by emissions from the local smelter in the past. These trees have done well in West Kootenay and Boundary, so well that they are endangering local forests and biodiversity ("Good Intentions Gone Bad").

The first name of his teacher, Robin, is there in the Latin genus name of this tree, *Robinia Pseudoacacia*. In this book, McGauley very often writes of this acacia, or false acacia: "acacia signified pollution reversed" (33), he remembers, its foliage disguising the original defoliation of the land-scape. From smelting came untold wealth but, he says, "That abundance alludes to acacia thorns" (38). The acacias were valued for roots that clutch loose soil, and that keep stony rubbish from slipping downhill or spreading in water. McGauley begins on waste grounds, even as he seeks to purge this setting of the slightest mystique: "Not where Rome meets campagna in black and white luminous wastelands but simply where we grew up" ("In river" 96).

Ezra Pound's influence is omnipresent in McGauley's poetry. The vine-stilled ship in Canto II is there in imagistic shorthand when he writes (as though visualizing an outboard motor in an overgrown yard): "Lynx steps, growls, then ivy over evinrude" (50). Pound's fascism is taken up in a reply to him ("re: Canto CXIII") in the first book of *Recarving the Chrysoprase Bowl*:

> Mia Battaglia mein kleiner
> Stumpf, o sweet Alabama
> his small light
>   utterly
> erased, obliterated, negated (185).

But later, the myth of his authority seems to cast its spell on its antagonist, McGauley. Pound's complicity with Mussolini's regime, beneath criticism, is blasted by bolts of invective. This invective calls to mind the crudeness of Cantos XIII-XV. On one hand, repetitious smashing of his name and image confirm the power of Pound's example for the poetics of *Recarving the Chrysoprase Bowl*. On the other, assurance that his "small light" lies, not only "erased", but also "obliterated", and not only "erased, obliterated" but (on top of that) "negated", suggests that iconoclastic reduction is less a matter of expediency than an end in its own right. The exposure of what is wrongly revered becomes an enabling condition of movement that drives the sequence forward.

Into the maelstrom of McGauley's Poundian invective fall many names, often surfacing just long enough to sink beneath it. Martin Heidegger is scourged as an enabler of Nazism, but the resistant detail of his thought is sidelined or ignored. He and Pound, compromised by fascism, are verbally bulldozed into closeness to its worse demagogue:

"Von Hindenburg's little brown uniformed shyster hallowed in ezratics, deep vomit in the nose". Yeats, scarcely even a phantom presence in *Recarving the Chrysoprase Bowl*, materializes in the third volume just long enough to be lashed for his affiliation with Eoin O'Duffy's militia, the Blueshirts ("COME HERE" 70). There is no wall, McGauley argues, between poetry and its lowest and most damning real-world entanglements. The idea of poetry's autonomy becomes an idol to fling down. But in the process, that with which poetry compromises, the political, is often reduced and simplified to a fabric of analogues, parallels, echoes, subject rhymes, interjections, and crude non sequiturs. This means that *Recarving the Chrysoprase Bowl* both is, and is not, a poem including history (as Pound's definition of epic puts it). The history included in it is, all too often, truncated, recast in the negative as a missile to hurl against believers in poetry's purity and authority, hence not included at all in a form equal to the density of its actual detail.

5. India and Carved Space

Recarving the Chrysoprase Bowl turns, time and again, back to the events of the summer of 1962.[7] This is the context of the night that McGauley remembers early in the sequence and then again, with intensified vividness, in the second volume: "On Hope's land, while fire-blackened marshmallows on sticks cooled from molten, with buttered corn on the cob, Ross heard bombs' thump" ("In river" 117). The coziness of this childhood idyll dissolves, then, in the same way that, later, his warm enthusiasm for the Doukhobor cause would subside into analytical coolness. The flow-paths of this movement, from forsaken zeal to sober atheism, spread throughout the sequence, studiously unearthed under a multiplicity of cultural forms. McGauley seems to say that the abolition of pseudo-spiritual illusions, under the right circumstances, can be fecundating and creative: "Such is absence formed from hope's nothing" (86). The words "absence formed" might identify the active verb in the title of *Recarving the Chrysoprase Bowl*. What else is made, by a carver's cut, than a carving, and what is a carved-out hollow but an "absence formed"? Carving, then, creation by subtraction, making by undoing, is

---

7   This was, in the epithet applied to it by Woodcock and Avakumovic, the "classic year of terrorist activity" in the Kootenays, "with an estimated total of 274 depredations" (350). See Holt 1964, pp. 187-193.

central to the life of his poetry, and the material of this undoing is, very often, "Hope's land", spiritual illusions that founder, the mystique of misplaced hopes that dies hard, under the chisel of a bleak artisanship.

To this artisanship belongs a natural affinity with iconoclasm, or image-smashing. But then, as the first book of *Recarving the Chrysoprase Bowl* nears its end, McGauley writes, in the imperative: "carve that music | paint mahadevis [sic] dancing" (218). He is, seemingly, thinking of the iconography of Śiva's dance of bliss, his *ānandatāṇḍava* or *tāṇḍava*. In this poem, then, carving is linked, not to icon-breaking but to icon-making. McGauley may have been to the temple complex at Cidambaram in Tamil Nadu, and seen its sculpture of the dancing Śiva, famous above all others (Johnson 18). His travels also took him to a place where carving, answering to cosmic and devotional ends, had taken the earth's surface as the medium of its activity. "At Ellora", he writes, "unremitting labour gives escarpment shape, restless, grasping, invisible, giving silence centuries later haunted resolution" ("In river" 49). The Caves of Ellora are cut in a bare rock face that extends for two kilometres. There are a great number, and many are not caves but immense temple interiors, several floors high, with courtyards open to the sky. The temples are Buddhist, Hindu, and Jain. It is the first that McGauley seems intent on foregrounding:

> Impregnable absolute already devoid of devotion, where now only the curious hungry walk through carved rock worshipped by bats' sonar, Buddhas set back in endless emptiness, a surfeit of credible absence, presence one endows, knee's patina showing hands' attention ("In river" 49).

A trace of the sacred attaches to the very silence that had seemed to signify its long absence. If not divine grace there is, writes McGauley, "graciousness" abounding there, even to the least receptive of its potential takers:

> Then hungry carved silent Ellora's graciousness, divine physiognomy foraging dubious credo to stave off oblivion. Careful to reassure when you think you have taken yourself away this curtails further doubt or at least puts back, wrapped up, stored not deeply, doubt's small machine capable of reactivation ("In river" 49).

It is not that this space silences doubt and places it in deep storage. Instead, carving on a sublime scale seems to both still and to sharpen doubt, laying it to rest but to awaken it to a keener alertness.

The most visited site at Ellora is the Kailash Temple, named after the mythical home of Śiva atop Mount Kailash, in Tibet. In sheer size, and in the profusion of its statues, pillars, and reliefs, this temple overshadows all those nearby it. "Architecturally, and sculpturally, this is undoubtedly the finest cave temple in the world", states one expert, only to retract its designation as a "cave temple": it is, he writes, better "described as a monolithic shrine – an architectural sculpture" (Dhavalikar 41, 42). This site in its entirety is consecrated to the power of Śiva. "In general", writes W. J. Johnson, "his representations in painting, sculpture, and narrative are intended to evoke the ambiguity in his power" (300), which is both infinitely destructive and cosmic in its creativity. The practice of architecture-in-the-negative, excavating instead of constructing, almost seems set apart by its nature to do homage to the power that makes as it takes away, creating as it destroys. "Impregnable absolute" no more, this power's cultic identity might still persist, and be felt, in the pregnant "silence" of the air that the voice of McGauley's memory describes. "Yes carved stone's godlike propensity" he assents, as though unwillingly or wearily ("In river" 164), late in the second book of *Recarving the Chrysoprase Bowl.*

The symbolism of Śiva is nothing if not profuse and complex. One element of this symbolism that fascinates McGauley is the story of the fall of the Ganges River. A hymn he adapts "after Cuntaram", i.e., Cuntarar or Sundarar, a Śivaite poet-saint, begins as follows (it is in this book):

> through his slowing hair
>
> Ganga falls to pool
>
> unselfconsciously
>
> he drinks
>
> poison
>
> his neck is
>
> blue he is
>
> dusty with

cremation ash (273).

The Ganges falls on the head of Śiva, who breaks its fall. His locks, clotted with ash, slow its currents and sift its waters. In *Recarving the Chrysoprase Bowl*, the poison-drinking, polluted Columbia River is a companion waterway to the Ganges. The poet-sage Basava (c.1106-1167) calls Śiva the "Lord of the Meeting Rivers" (Johnson 45), and McGauley inserts this epithet, to very different effect, in one of his own poems: "Said to their Lord of the Meeting Rivers, *come talk to me handsome*." Flirtatious abandon consorts, profanely, with premonitions of impending darkness. "Dark river's one is all, answers all, so said Cuntaram in Tamil" ("What is Given" 42, 46), or so McGauley remembers this saying. He also calls Śiva "Cuntaram's Blue Skinned One, dark lord of the 5 rivers" ("In river" 19). This tradition's representations associate his dance of bliss with the rotation of the cosmos from one cycle into another. The Śiva who dances this dance is known as Natarāja, or the Lord of the Dance (Johnson 42, 218). Statues and paintings depict him both poised and balanced, yet in furious motion. This iconography of active stillness, stasis in action, seems to enter *Recarving the Chrysoprase Bowl* as the thought that change is constant, and nothing abides. That McGauley returns to this same thought so often is a sign that something autotelic and self-determining inheres in it for him. This something might, then, be the residual afterglow of the sacred, represented as a force of perpetual change, of violent undoings and vital becomings.

If the dance of Śiva is a coinherence of making and undoing, then so is the humble handiwork of George Padowinikoff, who sits with a litter of shavings in his lap in *The Divine Comedy in Castlegar B.C.*, carving a spoon. A more unlikely partnering than this one is hard to imagine. Still, McGauley's poetry might suggest a coming together of some aesthetic values he associates with Doukhobor material culture, and others with the fane of Śiva he had been in at the site of the Ellora Caves. If the first is relentlessly minimalist, subject to an iconoclastic image-ban, the second is endlessly productive of ornate image-making. McGauley's poetics is, on one hand, austerely intransigent in its exclusion or minimization of narration, description, and personal self-disclosure. This asceticism means that he is close in spirit to the work of other poets associated with the New American Poetry, especially Olson and Blaser. But then, he also dissents from the magian and shamanic turn taken by his precursors, not to mention the politics of their elders. The need to expose misplaced hopes and cruel delusions motivates drastic measures that sometimes suggest iconoclasm. McGauley writes, in his words, "for and against the poets" ("Auburn bed" 24). But on the other hand, his poetry abounds to repletion with florid involutions and baroque lexical assemblages. In *Recarving the Chrysoprase Bowl* the auto-biographical is refracted through recalcitrant concretions of language. McGauley's life's work is not a universal mythography, on the model of Olson's *The Maximus Poems*, but a compacted record of travels, readings, and experiences. Ralph Maud, in a letter to Anne Carson (3 July 2001) calls him "a stern and marvelous poet in his own right".

Luke Franklin

Works Cited

Program for Ralph Maud's *The Divine Comedy in Castlegar B.C.* at the Images Theatre, Simon Fraser University, Vancouver. 1975.

Barker, John. Introduction. *The Bella Coola Indians*, by T.F. McIlwraith. Vol. 1, University of Toronto Press, 1992.

Cran, Gregory J. *Negotiating Buck Naked: Doukhobors, Public Policy, and Conflict Resolution*. University of British Columbia Press, 2006.

Charters, John. "Alexander Zuckerberg – From Dream to Reality." *British Columbia Historical News: Journal of the B.C. Historical Federation*, vol. 30, no. 3, 1997, pp. 26-28.

Dhavalkar, Madhukar Keshav. *Ellora: Monumental Legacy*. Oxford University Press, 2003.

Dorn, Edward. *Two Interviews*. Edited by Justin Katko and Gavin Selerie, Shearsman Books, 2012.

Fawcett, Brian. "How I Got a New American Education." *Minutes of the Charles Olson Society*, no. 51, 2003, pp. 3-13.

Federation of British Columbia Naturalists. "Good Intentions Gone Bad: A slow release bomb that will devastate our forests is exploding in the West Kootenay and Boundary Regions of B.C.", https://bcnature.org/wp-content/uploads/2022/02/Black-locust4.pdf. Accessed 24 Mar. 2025.

Holt, Simma. *Terror in the Name of God: The Story of the Sons of Freedom Doukhobors*. McClelland and Stewart Limited, 1964.

Johnson, W. J. *A Dictionary of Hinduism*. First ed., Oxford University Press, 2009.

Maude, Aylmer. *A Peculiar People: The Doukhobors*. Funk & Wagnalls Company, 1904.

Maud, Ralph. *Divine Comedy and Other Films*. 1977.

——. Letter to Anne Carson. 3 July 2001. Typescript.

McGauley, Tom. "COME HERE LONE SOLDIER. RCB3." Manuscript. 2024.

——. "Deer Park." *Serious Iron,* special issue of *Iron*, no. 2, 1971.

——. "In river never ending. Recarving the Chrysoprase Bowl: Selected Prose Poems. RCB2." Galleon Books, forthcoming.

——. Interview. Conducted by Melissa Allingham, 1993.

——. "In the auburn bed of righteous adventure: RCB4." Manuscript. 2023

——. Letter to Fred Makortoff. 18 March 1983. Typescript.

——. "'or, 'The Going-On.'" *The Peak,* 17 Feb. 1971, p. 17.

——. "Quick notes on RCB3: COME HERE LONE SOLDIER. 29.04.24." Manuscript. 2024.

——. "She said it was anger." *West Coast Line: A Journal of Contemporary Writing and Criticism*, no. 1, spring 1990, pp. 56.

——. Statement on Poetics. *West Coast Line: A Journal of Contemporary Writing and Criticism*, no. 1, spring 1990, pp. 134-137.

——. "What is Given. RCB4." Manuscript. 2024.

McIlwraith, T. F. *The Bella Coola Indians.* Vol. 1, University of Toronto Press, 1992.

Murphy, Patrick D. "Damning damming modernity: the destructive role of Megadams." *Tamkang Review*, vol. 42, no. 1, 2011, pp. 27-40.

Nixon, Rob. "Unimagined Communities: Developmental Refugees, Megadams, and Monumental Modernity." *New Formations*, no. 69, 2009, pp. 62-80.

Pearkes, Eileen Delehanty. *A River Captured: The Columbia River Treaty and Catastrophic Change.* Rocky Mountain Books, 2024.

Pryce, Paula. *"Keeping the Lakes' Way": Reburial and the Re-creation of a Moral World Among an Invisible People.* University of Toronto Press, 1999.

Prynne, J.H. "On Maximus IV, V, VI", *Serious Iron,* special issue of *Iron*, no. 2, 1971.

Ramanujan, A.K. Introduction. *Hymns for the Drowning: Poems for Viṣṇu by Nammāḻvār*, translated by Ramanujan, Princeton University Press, 1981, pp. ix-xviii.

Van Hallberg, Robert. *Charles Olson: The Scholar's Art.* Harvard University Press, 1978.

Wilson, James Wood. *People in the Way: The Human Aspects of the Columbia River Project.* University of Toronto Press, 2019.

Woodcock, George, and Ivan Avakumovic. *The Doukhobors*, Oxford University Press, 1968.

Postscript: September 2025

"Prune apricot so that it blossom" writes McGauley (257). This is the adage of a poet who writes but to revise, and practices revision as composition: only on condition of taking care to cut back, to prune, to clip out, to do away with, is anything done for whatever, in a poem, might count as its shoots, its bud-bearing spurs. Pruning is arboreally what carving is in the sculptor's studio: an art of taking out, of creation through subtraction. All this going back, to take out, consumes time, and this book, long in the making, was to come out after McGauley's death. In the last week of July 2025 he passed away at his home in Burnaby, British Columbia, where he had lived for many years. He is survived by his partner, his sisters, nephews, nieces, a wide circle of friends, and by his poetry, his life's work.

Tom McGauley was born in British Columbia in 1948 and grew up in Castlegar. A student of Robin Blaser, Ralph Maud, and Jerry Zaslove, at Simon Fraser University, he was also a scholar of local history and Doukhobor life in the Kootenays. He served on the executive of his union (CUPE Local 379) and on many boards in his community —the Burnaby Public Library Board of Trustees, the City of Burnaby's Visual Arts Advisory Board, and the Burnaby Parks and Recreation Commission. The many-sided sense of connection he had with India and its traditions was a strong influence on his writing and his feeling for history. *Recarving the Chrysoprase Bowl* is his life's work, a poem in several books, under revision and in the making for many years.

Luke Franklin is Associate Fellow in the Contemporary Studies Program, University of King's College, Halifax, Nova Scotia.

www.ingramcontent.com/pod-product-compliance
Lightning Source LLC
Chambersburg PA
CBHW071706120626
46550CB00001B/128